Ardell Winters

Transcribed by Diane Narlock
Edited by Brad Shirley

Copyright © 2013 Dr. Leonard Gardner
All rights reserved.
ISBN-10: 1484942396
ISBN-13: 978-1484942390

Favorites

Best Loved Sermons from 60+ Years of Ministry

Dr. Leonard Gardner

2013

Favorites

Best Loved Sermons from 60+ Years of Ministry

Table of Contents

Introduction

For a number of years, I have had the privilege of traveling throughout the United States and Canada, teaching and preaching God's Word. During that time, I have been blessed to meet many dedicated pastors, committed leaders, and precious men and women who truly love God and His Word. Over the course of time, people have voiced their desire to have some of my messages in book form. This book, simply called "Favorites," represents a number of messages that people have identified as those that have impacted their lives to a significant degree. My sincere desire is that you will be blessed and encouraged in your relationship with our Lord Jesus Christ as you enjoy these favorites from the wonderful, life-giving Word of God.

Behold My Son

The Book of Matthew records an event which occurred during the middle of the earthly ministry of Jesus which, in my opinion, was one of the key points in His ministry. Matthew 12:9-14 contains the account of Jesus healing a man with a withered hand in the synagogue and shortly thereafter, according to Matthew 12:15, "he (Jesus) withdrew himself from thence; and great multitudes followed him, and he healed them all." Please note the word "all" in this scripture. Every single person that followed Jesus that day was healed of his or her affliction!

Matthew goes on to write (Matthew 12:17-21) that Jesus' healing of *all* of the people was the fulfillment of a prophecy that God had spoken through the prophet Isaiah seven hundred fifty years earlier. Isaiah 42:1-3 declares, "Behold my servant, whom I uphold; mine elect, in whom my soul delighteth; I have put my spirit upon him: he shall bring forth judgment to the Gentiles. He shall not cry, nor lift up, nor cause his voice to be heard in the street. A bruised reed shall he not break, and the smoking flax shall he not quench: he shall bring forth judgment unto truth." Please note that in Isaiah's prophecy, when God the Father spoke of His "servant," He was referring to His Son, Jesus Christ.

Behold!

God was effectively saying through Isaiah, "First and foremost, I want you to behold My Son." The Hebrew word translated "behold" is very significant. It does not mean simply to glance at or look upon, then turn away. The word translated "behold" is a very strong word which means "to focus on; to stare at and not take your eyes off." God the Father was saying, "Behold My Son. I want to tell you some things about My Son." The Father was excited about His Son seven hundred

Favorites – Best Loved Sermons from 60+ Years of Ministry

fifty years before Jesus came to earth!

Most parents are excited about their children and enjoy talking about their children's abilities or accomplishments. We have all seen bumper stickers such as "Proud Parent of a Sixth Grade Honor Student." God the Father also loves to speak about His Son. The Father tells us through the prophet Isaiah that it is important that we put our eyes on ("behold") His Son.

Because the Father called attention to His Son with the word "Behold," we might expect Him to speak about the great things His Son would do. Perhaps He would say, "My Son is going to walk on water and turn water into wine. He is going to multiply bread and fish. My Son is even going to raise people from the dead!" However, Father didn't speak of the _acts_ of His Son, as impressive as they were, but instead, Father spoke of the _heart_ of His Son.

God revealed to Matthew that Jesus healing them _all_ was a fulfillment of Isaiah's prophecy in which God declared, regarding His Son, "A bruised reed shall he not break, and the smoking flax shall he not quench; he shall bring forth judgment unto truth." (Isaiah 42:3) The word translated "truth" in this verse can be literally translated as "victory." Therefore, Matthew 12:20 quotes Isaiah's prophecy as "....he shall bring forth judgment unto victory."

Father was effectively saying, "Behold My Son, because He will not break a bruised reed, and He will not quench smoking flax." This is the _because_ that followed the _all_ healing. In other words, Jesus healed them _all_ that it might be fulfilled what God had effectively said through Isaiah, "Behold My Son, who will not break a bruised reed nor quench smoking flax."

The meaning of the phrases "bruised reed" and "smoking flax" are not commonplace knowledge in our modern Western world. In order to recognize the significance of what God was saying, we must understand customs and practices in Bible times. Understanding this will help us as we anticipate, and prepare for, what I believe is a coming great move of God, which I will call the "all move of God" in which, I believe, there will be times when all that are gathered together in a given place are healed by the power of God. Father declared, "A bruised reed He will not break." What is the significance of a bruised reed?

Three Kinds of Reeds

There were three kinds of reeds in Bible times. The first was called a *common reed*. It was a plant that grew to about twelve feet in height but was not prevalent or plentiful. The second type of reed was *papyrus*. It was unique in that it had very strong roots of about twenty feet in length. Papyrus reeds were plentiful along the Nile River in Egypt.

The third kind of reed, and the one on which we will focus, was called the *bulrush*. Bulrushes were plentiful in the Jordan Valley along the Jordan River, and around the Dead Sea. A number of bulrushes growing together would create a dense field of heavy brush. Bulrushes could grow to eighteen feet in height. The base of the trunk, which could be as thick as three inches in diameter, was filled with pith, a dry and spongy tissue.

Bulrushes

The account of baby Moses in Exodus Chapter 2 contains references to both papyrus and bulrushes. When Pharaoh decreed that all young Hebrew male children were to be killed, a Hebrew woman named Jochebed hid her young son Moses from the Egyptian authorities for three months in order to save his life. She then made an ark (a basket) by weaving bulrushes together, and she sealed the ark with slime and pitch. She placed little Moses in the ark and hid him among the papyrus along the banks of the Nile River.

Bulrushes were very important to the lifestyle of the Hebrews in that day. They used bulrushes to make walking canes, writing instruments, handles for farming implements, and kitchen utensils. They also used bulrushes to make reed instruments, which were important in the lives and work of shepherds.

The Shepherd's Music

Shepherds spent many hours out in the fields tending their sheep, and they often played reed instruments that were made from bulrushes. Their sheep became very accustomed to the variety of sounds that the shepherd made with the instrument, and the shepherd could actually communicate with the sheep through the music. By certain specific sounds the shepherd would make with the instrument, the sheep knew, for example, that it was time to eat or time to bed down. The sheep knew the shepherd was near when they heard the soothing and peaceful sounds of the instrument, and it brought them comfort.

Making the Instrument

The process of making reed instruments required patience and skill. First, a sharp knife was used to cut off a piece of a bulrush and then hollow it out by digging out the pith inside. Then, the knife was used to cut holes in the reed at properly spaced intervals to affect the flow of air and therefore create a variety of notes and sounds.

The process required delicate work with the knife in the cutting of the reed, the hollowing out, and the cutting of the holes. It was fairly common for the instrument makers to make mistakes in the process. Perhaps the bulrush had been not cut cleanly, a piece had broken off, or it had split as a result of hollowing it out. When a mistake was made in the process, the bulrush would be discarded instead of being repaired because bulrushes were so plentiful. The instrument maker would simply cut off another piece of bulrush and start over. Because of this, a person walking along the Jordan or around the Dead Sea might see many discarded reeds strewn all over the ground. These discarded bulrushes were referred to as *bruised reeds* and were considered useless. Therefore, people would kick them around, step on them, or disregard them entirely.

Bruised Reeds

In the process of the making, the bruised reeds that had been marred in some way were considered to be useless refuse of no worth or value. I believe that this speaks to us of people that have been bruised in the process of the making, and who, as a consequence, have either been discarded, cast aside, rejected, ignored, stepped on, or considered worthless.

Our world is filled with people who are "bruised reeds." If we open our spiritual eyes and look at the people all around us, we will likely see wounded and hurting people who are considered worthless by society and/or themselves. However, God the Father effectively says, "I want to tell you about My Son. He doesn't see people as worthless or hopeless. He doesn't see junk. He sees potential. He doesn't step on them, break them, or kick them out of the way. He doesn't ignore them or reject them. He stops and picks them up. A bruised reed He will not break. He commits Himself to restore that bruised reed to such an extent that it will make beautiful music once again in the hand of the Master."

Luke 4:18 records the first sermon that Jesus preached at Nazareth, which speaks of His heart for the broken and bruised. Jesus said, "The Spirit of the Lord is upon me, because he hath anointed me to preach the gospel to the poor; He hath sent me to heal the brokenhearted, to preach deliverance to the captives, and recovering of sight to the blind, to set at liberty them that are bruised." He will not discard nor break a bruised reed!

The Reeds and Jesus

Mark 15:19 provides an interesting detail when it states that, at Jesus' trial, the Roman soldiers smote Him on the head with a reed. It is as if Satan was saying, "Take that, you who will not step on a reed! You who will not brush aside a reed. You who will not reject a reed. Take this pain from a reed." Also, Mark 15:36 records the account when Jesus was on the cross and the soldiers soaked a sponge in vinegar, put it on the end of a reed, and tried to make Jesus drink from it. In so doing, the enemy was using reeds to mock the one that would not break a bruised reed.

If we are Christians, it is because one day, somewhere, somehow, in each of our lives, Jesus walked by and looked at us as we were lying there rejected, broken, distressed, and bleeding inside. We were seemingly useless, hopeless, and unwanted, but He saw potential. He didn't see what we were; He saw what we were going to be. He didn't focus on the fact that someone made a mistake and marred us during the making process. Human beings make mistakes with their "sharp knives" (actions and words) and therefore bruise other human beings. We all are bruised at times and feel discarded, but Jesus effectively says, "I'm going to make sweet music with your life, because there are sheep out there on the hillside that will hear the sound and understand it and come to the Good Shepherd. I'm going to heal them and make shepherds out of some of them such that they themselves will have the privilege of calling the sheep."

How great is the glory, grace, and might of our Lord! He has chosen to show us favor, and He has poured out His love upon us. Only He can understand how He could love someone so marred and bruised. "A bruised reed shall he not break." Now that we understand this truth, we can begin to understand why Jesus looked at the multitude (Matthew 12:15) and knew that there were none that couldn't be fixed. He is looking out on the world today, into every troubled heart and mind, knowing that there are none that can't be fixed, changed, and made new. A bruised reed He will not break!

A Smoking Flax

In Isaiah's prophecy, the Father effectively said that He is not only excited about the way His Son treats the bruised reeds, but also that His Son will not quench smoking flax. Flax is a flowering plant that grows up to five feet in height. As flax begins to mature, it develops small capsules called bolls on the stem. When a farmer sees the stem filled with bolls, he knows that the flax is mature and ready to be harvested and processed.

The same Hebrew word for "flax" also means "wicks." When the flax was mature, it was pulled up by the roots and laid out on the flat rooftops of houses to dry. Incidentally, according to Joshua 2:6, the two Hebrew spies who were sent into Jericho were hidden by Rahab on her housetop under the flax. After the flax dried, it was bundled and then soaked in water for two to three weeks and, as it was soaking, it went through a process called retting. In the retting process, all of the fibers would separate such that they could actually be combed out. The finest of linen was made from the fibers that were produced by the retting process.

The fibers were also woven together to make wicks. Wicks were very important to everyday living in those times, to provide light and warmth. Their lamps consisted of an oil-filled pot with a wick inserted. The oil would travel up the wick, saturating it, and when lit, the lamp would give off both light and heat. The oil flowing through the wick burned, but the wick would not burn.

A Smoldering Wick

Sometimes, if a wick wasn't properly maintained or the pot lacked oil, it could start to burn. When a wick burnt, it gave off black smoke and emitted a foul odor that smelled like flesh.   When the housekeeper saw the black smoke and smelled the foul odor, they would discard the wick and replace it with another one. The smell of the smoldering wick was simply too putrid to bear.

God the Father says that He is proud of His Son because when He sees smoking flax and smells the stench of flesh, He doesn't discard it. Instead, He applies more oil. When the oil is back in the pot again, the wick comes alive and gives off light. Jesus said that we are the light of the world. He said, "Let your light so shine before men, that they may see your good works, and glorify your Father which is in heaven." (Matthew 5:16).   Jesus pours in the oil and will not throw the wick away. In Joel 2:28-29, God declares, "I will pour out my spirit upon all flesh and your sons and your daughters shall prophesy, your old men shall dream dreams, your young men shall see visions; And also upon the servants and upon the handmaids in those days will I pour out my spirit." Please note the words *spirit* and *flesh*. Oil is a type of the Holy Spirit, and through the prophet Joel, God effectively said that He would pour out the *oil* on all *flesh*.

When Jesus smells flesh, He doesn't discard it. Instead, He pours the oil. We need more oil when we begin to give off black smoke. Jesus won't break a bruised reed nor discard smoking flax because He is ministering in such a way to heal us all.   Father is proud of His Son because He heals all, including the bruised reeds and the smoking flax.

In Jesus' day, there were many religious people that were quenching smoking flax and simply throwing it out.   They were disqualifying people from a relationship with God and stoning them for their mistakes. They were telling people they didn't qualify, but along came Jesus to pour oil on _all_ flesh! The Spirit of grace, mercy, and power began to come forth. There is no one so badly bruised that He can't heal them. There is no flax, no wick that's gone so far that He will destroy it. It doesn't matter what you have been through. All you need to know is what He said. He will not break a bruised reed or quench a smoking flax!

Joel prophesied that our young men will prophesy and our old men will dream dreams. "Upon my servants and handmaids will I pour out my spirit, saith the Lord." (Joel 2:29) God is a restoring God. Jesus is effectively saying, "That smells like flesh but I'm not going to throw it away. I'm going to pour in the oil." I believe this will happen in the end time hour. I believe we're going to see a great move of the Spirit. I believe that God has poured His Spirit out upon us such that we have His heart for the people that are bruised reeds and smoking flax. In the same way that Father said "Behold My Son" because He was excited about Jesus' heart and His ministry to broken and hurting people, the Father will be pleased with us, as His sons and daughters, as we reach out to those that are bruised reeds and smoking flax.

The Best Man

John the Baptist was a man who represented the transition between the old and the new. He was very unique, yet called of God and anointed for the purpose he was to fulfill and to bring the message he was called to bring.

Early in the earthly ministry of Jesus, John the Baptist was baptizing people in water near a place called Bethabara, which was east of the Jordan and approximately directly east of Judea. During a baptism service one day, Jesus walked by and John interrupted what he was doing, pointed to Jesus, and said, "Behold the Lamb of God who taketh away the sin of the world." (John 1:29) Jesus walked on, and John resumed baptizing. A short time later, Jesus returned and asked John to baptize Him in water as well. John struggled at first with Jesus' request, but he then yielded and immersed Jesus in the waters of the Jordan.

When Jesus came up out of the water, the Holy Spirit in the form of a dove descended upon Jesus, and John specifically writes (John 1:32-33) that the dove _remained_ on Jesus. The fact that the Spirit remained on Him was significant, because no one up until that time could experience that. Prior to this time, the Holy Spirit would come upon people to empower them for a specific work or purpose and then would depart. However, Jesus was the only one who, as the Son of God, had pure, uncontaminated blood so the Holy Spirit could not only descend upon Him but also remain upon Him. The Spirit can never go where the blood hasn't already been.

Early in the first year of Jesus' earthly ministry, He and His disciples began to minister to the people in Bethabara. Jesus authorized His disciples to baptize the people that came to Him. John the Baptist was baptizing on the west side of the Jordan River in Aenon,

Favorites – Best Loved Sermons from 60+ Years of Ministry

about seventy-five to ninety miles northeast of where Jesus was. At that particular time, Jesus only had five of the twelve that would ultimately be called His disciples. There was Andrew, Peter, Philip, and Nathanael, and the fifth is unnamed. The crowds began to increase and it wasn't long before there were more people coming to Bethabara to be baptized by Jesus' disciples than were going up to be baptized by John the Baptist.

John the Baptist's Disciples' Complaint

Jesus' popularity continued to grow until one day the disciples of John the Baptist came to John, apparently upset. John 3:26 states, "And they came unto John, and said unto him, Rabbi, he that was with thee beyond Jordan (now they are talking about Jesus), to whom thou barest witness (because he said behold the Lamb of God about Him), behold, the same baptizeth, and all men come to him." Please note that it states that *all men* were coming to Him.

John's disciples were troubled because they perceived John was losing popularity and effectively losing his "number one" status as the baptizer. "John, how can this be? Baptism is *our* ministry. Why is Jesus doing our ministry? You introduced Him and now He is taking over." John must have thought, "Why are they so upset simply because Jesus is baptizing and people are going to Him instead of me?" I believe that John's disciples were struggling with what sports psychiatrists call "reflected glory" which means that if you can't be the "top dog" yourself, you want to be associated with the one that is the top dog. If the one you are associated with is "slipping in the ratings," it has a negative effect on your self-esteem and your pride. John's disciples were troubled about what was happening.

I am certain that the enemy wanted to abort John's ministry, and perhaps he tried to get John to think, "If Jesus is doing better than I am, perhaps I should alter my ministry." Perhaps one of John's disciples even had some suggestions. "John, you must modify your message if you want more people to come. I have heard that many people aren't happy about the repentance message that you have been preaching. And, remember that sermon you preached entitled 'Generation of Vipers?' People didn't react favorably to that! John, you should dress a little better and mind your manners. It's not attractive when locusts are hanging out of your mouth and your camel hair garment is worn and dirty. John, we must do something about your public image. If we don't do something, even more people will be leaving us and flocking to Jesus."

Perhaps John was tempted to consider Jesus as a competitor and become angry with Him. It is possible that the enemy was trying to subtly strip John's ministry from him. I am grateful that John did not yield to any apparent temptations. He didn't modify his message. There is no evidence he changed his dress. There is absolutely no proof that he ever opposed Jesus or considered Him an enemy. John simply kept doing what God had called him to do. He continued to be what God had told him to be, and God therefore continued to use him in a very unique ministry.

John the Baptist's Response

I believe John's disciples were trying to deal with something supernatural in a natural way. They were trying to address something that was not a problem at all. I love John's answer to his disciples, and I believe that his words convey to us principles that are very important in every one of our lives.

John 3:27 states, "John answered, and said, A man can receive nothing, except it be given him from heaven." He was effectively saying that his disciples should not be upset about the fact that Jesus was baptizing more people than he, or that Jesus had more people at His gatherings, because no one can have anything unless God gives it to him. If God has anointed someone, we should embrace it even if what they have is unlike what we have, or if they are drawing more attention. John was saying that Jesus' ministry was not something with which John and his disciples should contend, but rather they should see it is a complement to their ministry. This is a very important truth to embrace. John effectively said, "Jesus has His baptizing ministry because the Father gave it to Him, and because of it, the kingdom of God is stronger now. The kingdom of God is more powerful now. The kingdom of God has been enhanced. Let us rejoice."

Knowing Our Place

John 3:28 declares, "Ye yourselves bear me witness that I said; I am not the Christ, but that I am sent before him." There are two key phrases in that sentence. One phrase is "I am not," and the other phrase is "I am." It's very important to not only know *who we are*, but it's also important to know *who we are not*. John had that clearly sorted out. He was effectively saying, "I am not the Christ. I told you that before. I am the one sent before Him. I have a purpose and a specific calling, but I'm not in competition with anyone. I'm simply here to obey and fulfill what I'm called to do, and what I'm called to be. Therefore, it is important that I know *who I am not* as well as *who I am*."

For a number of years in my ministry, I wanted so badly to sing. I kept trying to sing, but it took me a long time to realize that I am not a singer. Thank the Lord that He raised up my children who can sing. Our church didn't start growing until I stopped singing. You can relax in what you are if you know what you are not. You don't have to keep striving, worrying, and working to be what you are not.

We must each know our place. Some people continually try to be who they are not, and in doing so, they are not being who they really are. We are each unique to God and we each have something to give. He loves us and He made us just like we are. John the Baptist understood this truth. He didn't have to modify his message, change his clothes, or be concerned about the number of people that were following Jesus instead of him. John made it clear that he knew who he was and what his purpose was, and that he wasn't the Christ. He wasn't trying to get his fulfillment from being someone he wasn't.

We will only be truly fulfilled when we are who we were called to be. I frequently tell people, "Be real and be yourself. God made you the way He made you for a reason. Be yourself. Everyone else is taken." Someone else's anointing or calling is no threat to you but rather a complement to accomplishing the work of the Lord. We should work together, embrace one another, strengthen one another, and encourage one another. We will see the glory of God manifested as we are who He has called us to be.

The Shoshbin, Friend of the Bridegroom

John continued, as recorded in John 3:29, "He that hath the bride is the bridegroom, but the friend of the bridegroom, which standeth and heareth him, rejoiceth greatly because of the bridegroom's voice; this my joy therefore is fulfilled." John's statement was simple and powerful. The bride is one of the types and one of the symbols of the church and of the Christian. First, John was saying that *the bride belongs to the bridegroom*. Secondly, John effectively said that he received his joy and fulfillment by being who he was called to be, which basically meant being obedient to the one that called him. He had no desire to try to get his joy from what someone else was called to be.

John was also saying that *he was a friend of the bridegroom*. The bride is the church, the bridegroom is Christ, and John is a friend of the bridegroom. In Bible days, the most important person in a wedding party, except for the bride and bridegroom, was called "the friend of the bridegroom" and the title given to him was the *Shoshbin*. John was effectively saying, "I am a Shoshbin, Jesus is the bridegroom, and the people of God are the bride. As a Shoshbin, I have a very important part to play in the entire purpose of Almighty God." The Shoshbin had three primary responsibilities in a wedding.

Sending Out the Invitations

The Shoshbin's first responsibility was to send out the invitations. He was the one that ensured that the people who were to be invited to the wedding feast had received an invitation and were aware of the time and the place. John the Baptist is the first of the Shoshbins, as are we, who are called to be an important part of the marriage supper of the Lamb (Revelation 19:9). One of our responsibilities as a Shoshbin is to issue an invitation to everyone we meet to come to the marriage supper of the Lamb. We invite them to repent and make Jesus Christ the Lord of their lives and, when they do, the consequence is that their sins are remitted and they become part of the eternal family of God. As good Shoshbins, that is one of our principle responsibilities.

In 2012, my wife went home to be with the Lord. If I've ever seen a person that was always passing out invitations, it was her. Once, I went to the hospital to visit her and she wasn't in her room, so I started down the hallway to look for her. Sure enough, there she was with her I.V. pole, going from room to room telling people about Jesus. She was being a Shoshbin in that hospital. Just a few days before she passed, she was very sick and several nurses were attending to her. One of the nurses said something about wine. She looked up at them and said, "Have you heard about the new wine?" She was passing out invitations. She simply wanted to be a Shoshbin.

Bringing the Bride Closer to the Bridegroom

The second responsibility of the Shoshbin was that, when the marriage supper had been prepared, he was to go to the bride's house and personally accompany her to the marriage supper, where the bridegroom was waiting for her. In accompanying her, he had two responsibilities. One was to keep her from becoming distracted by other things along the way, and the second was to protect her and keep her from danger or harm. Therefore, the Shoshbin was responsible to bring the bride closer to the bridegroom. It was his responsibility to bring the bride to the bridegroom so that they could be one forevermore.

John was effectively saying to his disciples, "The reason you're upset is because you think that we're in competition with Jesus, but we are not. That's not what I'm all about. I am here to bring the bride to the bridegroom." That's a very simple but important part of the call on every single one of us as believers. Regardless of our title or giftings, our charge is to bring people closer to Jesus so they see Him, praise Him, want more of Him, and want to glorify Him.

If the result of my writing this book is that you love Jesus more and your commitment to Him becomes deeper, then I have been a faithful Shoshbin. That's all I am. My title is not important nor is my name. My function as a Shoshbin is to bring you closer to Jesus. It's all about Him.

We all can become distracted with other things, but the Shoshbin's job is to keep the bride from getting distracted or harmed until he can present her to the bridegroom. It's not about us. It's all about Him. Our charge, our call, the reason we're anointed, the reason we're gifted, the reason we have anything we have, is to glorify Him. It's all about Him. The Word is all about Him. The books of the Bible are named differently but they are all about Him. From beginning to end, we will never understand the Word until we understand it's all about Him.

I've seen people struggling for years over the book of Revelation trying to argue about the third finger on the left foot of the beast, but they haven't moved past the first five words of the book. It is the revelation of Jesus Christ. It's all about Jesus. Knowing this dissolves jealousies, strife, and contention. John the Baptist's disciples were upset because they didn't understand that it's all about Jesus. John was effectively saying, "We're not competing with His baptizing to see who has the largest number of people being baptized. We are here to bring people closer to Him."

That's the way I feel about myself. I don't care if people ever know me. I just want everyone that crosses my path to want more of Jesus. One of these days I will bow out of the picture and rejoice as the bride and the bridegroom come together. I simply want to be a Shoshbin.

Jesus in the New Testament

I see Jesus in every book of the New Testament. In Matthew, He's the Messiah. In Mark, He's the Miracle Worker. In Luke, He's the Son of Man. In John, He's the Son of God. In Acts, He's the Name Above Every Other Name. In Romans, He's Our Justification. In I Corinthians, He is Our Resurrection. In II Corinthians, He's Our Sin-bearer. In Galatians, He's the Redeemer from the Curse of the Law. In Ephesians, He is the Unsearchable Riches Of God. In Philippians, He is the Supplier of All Our Need. In Colossians, He is the Fullness of the Godhead Bodily. In Thessalonians, He is Our Soon Coming King. In Timothy, He is the Mediator Between God and Man. In Titus, He is Our Blessed Hope. In Philemon, He is a Friend that Sticketh Closer than a Brother. In Hebrews, He is the Blood of the Everlasting Covenant. In

James, He is the Lord Our Healer. In Peter, He is the Chief Shepherd. In John, He is the Lover of Our Souls. In Jude, He is the One that is Able to Keep Us from Falling and to Present Us Faultless Before His Throne with Exceeding Great Joy. In Revelation, He is the King of Kings and Lord of Lords. He's there in every single book. He is there. It's all about Jesus.

Jesus in the Old Testament

Just because there are no red letters in the Old Testament, it doesn't mean Jesus isn't there also. Jesus is there. He is concealed, but we see Him by revelation in the Old Testament. The Old Testament has been referred to as "Jesus concealed" and the New Testament as "Jesus revealed." The entire Bible is all about Jesus. Proverbs 25:2 declares, "It is the glory of God to conceal a thing; but the honour of kings is to search out a matter." As we study the Word, we will find He's there. It's not about us; it's all about Him, and when we get our focus right, we can walk in peace, joy, and fulfillment because He will never change. We still stand in awe of Him. We still rejoice in awe of Him. We cannot wholly explain Him. Vocabulary bends its knee, unable to find the word to express who He is.

I open my Bible to the book of Genesis and He's there. He's the Creator, the Beginning, and the Word. In Exodus, He's the Passover Lamb. In Leviticus, He's the Great High Priest. In Numbers, He's the Pillar of Cloud by Day and the Pillar of Fire by Night. In Deuteronomy, He is the City of Refuge. In Joshua, He is the Courageous Conqueror. In Judges, He's the Lawgiver. In Ruth, He's the Kinsman Redeemer. In Samuel, He's the Trusted, True Prophet. In Kings and Chronicles, He is the Sovereign, Reigning, Eternal King Forevermore. In Ezra, He's the Trusted, True Scribe. In Nehemiah, He's the Rebuilder of Broken Walls and Broken Lives. In Esther, He is the Golden Scepter. In Job, He is the Redeemer That Ever Liveth. In Psalms, He's not only the Shepherd, but He is also the Song. In Proverbs, He is Our Wisdom. In Ecclesiastes, He's the Time and the Season. In Song of Solomon, He is the Beloved Bridegroom. In Daniel, He is the Fourth Man in the Fire. In Hosea, He is Married to the Backslider. In Joel, He is the Early Rain and the Latter Rain. In Amos, He is the Burden-bearer. In Obadiah, He is the Lord Our Deliverer. In Jonah, He is Our Savior Not Willing That Any Should

Perish. In Micah, He is the Promise Of Peace. In Nahum, He is Our Strength and Our Shield. In Habakkuk, He is the Vision of Things to Come. In Zephaniah, He is the Lord God, Mighty To Save. In Haggai, He is the Restorer of All Things That Were Lost. In Zechariah, He is the Fountain of Cleansing. In Malachi, He is the Son of Righteousness with Healing in His Wings. He is there! It's Jesus, Jesus, Jesus.

Making Way for the Bridegroom

The third thing for which the Shoshbin was responsible occurred on the final night of the wedding feast, which normally lasted seven days. At that time, the Shoshbin would usher the bride to the bridal tent, where she would await the coming of her bridegroom. The Shoshbin would stand outside the tent in the darkness of the night and protect the bride until he heard the voice of the bridegroom piercing the darkness. Note that the Shoshbin had to know the bridegroom's voice in order to recognize it. When he heard the voice of the bridegroom coming through the night to receive his bride, the Shoshbin would simply step out of the way and effectively say, "She doesn't belong to me, she belongs to you. I've simply been watching her for a season. I've been trying to keep her from getting distracted so she won't pursue things other than the bridegroom. I've been trying to keep her from harm and danger so she is preserved and whole in the eyes of the bridegroom." When the bridegroom's voice pierces the darkness and he comes for his bride, the Shoshbin's job is done.

The Best Man

I believe there is a reason that Jesus said in Matthew 11:11 that of all those born of women, John the Baptist rose to be the greatest. The word "rose" is *yergo* in the Greek language. It means "to come to a higher level." John had come to a higher place of understanding. He knew that there was no need for contention or competition. John effectively said, "I have the joy of the friend of the bridegroom, and you are not going to take my joy from me." He knew his place. He was the Shoshbin.

We call the Shoshbin the "Best Man" in our western culture.

The best man is not the bridegroom; he's the best man! This is the way I look at ministry. If I leave a deposit through my words that causes you to be hungry for more of Jesus, then I have done my job as the best man. It matters to me if the bride is closer to the Bridegroom. It matters to me if your hunger for the Word is growing and your heart longs for more of Him. I want to be a faithful Shoshbin. That's all that matters to me. One day He'll call me home, and the issue will be whether my being here, touching your life in some small way, made you want more of Jesus. That's my purpose and my passion.

I want to keep you from getting distracted because it's all about Him. I want to keep you from getting harmed or in danger because I believe that it won't be very long before the clouds are going to open up just like that bridegroom's voice came through the darkness on that wedding night. The Spirit and the Bride are going to say, "Come." (Revelation 22:17) The Bridegroom's voice will sound like trumpets, and He will say, "I'm here, time is no more." Until then, let's ask God to help us influence our friends, family, children, and neighbors in a way that they will closer to Jesus because of knowing us.

The Bible says something beautiful about Lazarus. The testimony of how he was raised from the dead concludes with the fact that because of Lazarus' resurrection, many people believed in Jesus. (John 11:45) That is a powerful testimony. Let it be said about each of us that because we lived, people were brought closer to Jesus and followed Him. God still chooses to preach His Word and spread the Gospel through Shoshbins, and being a Shoshbin is perhaps the highest calling in the whole world. We may be placed in a particular responsibility and we should execute it as faithfully as we can, but our fulfillment is found in Him and in obedience to what He's called us to do. May each of us be faithful Shoshbins, bringing people closer to Jesus in all that we do.

Blindness to Clear Sight

It is an interesting fact that many miracle accounts in the gospels record the healing of either the blind, the deaf, or the lame. The Bible tells us that Jesus healed all manner of diseases, and we know that there is no physical malady that He cannot heal. Yet, the Holy Spirit chose to record many miracles which specifically refer to the healing of the blind, the deaf, and the lame. I believe it's because there is spiritual significance and relevance in these miracles to all of us today. When Jesus opens the eyes of the blind, He is showing us that He wants us to be able to see as He sees. When He opens deaf ears, He is saying He wants us to be able to hear what the Spirit is saying to the churches. Healing the lame indicates that He wants us to learn how to walk as we should walk as Christians. He wants to help us see beyond the obvious and receive strength, direction, help, encouragement, and blessing in our lives today. I want to emphasize that I wholeheartedly believe in the literal interpretation of the Bible. I believe that during His earthly ministry, Jesus physically healed many blind, deaf, and lame people, and I believe the Holy Spirit recorded these specific accounts so that we can learn and apply truths and principles to our lives.

Let's examine the account of Jesus healing a blind man at Bethsaida and ask the Holy Spirit to reveal to us the truths that He wants us to learn and apply in our daily walk with Him. Mark 8:22-26 declares, "And he cometh to Bethsaida; and they bring a blind man unto him, and besought him to touch him. And he took the blind man by the hand, and led him out of the town; and when he had spit on his eyes, and put his hands upon him, he asked him if he saw ought. And he looked up, and said, I see men as trees, walking. After that he put his hands again upon his eyes, and made him look up; and he was

19   Favorites – Best Loved Sermons from 60+ Years of Ministry

restored, and saw every man clearly. And he sent him away to his house, saying, Neither go into the town, nor tell it to any in the town."

Bethsaida

I believe that every time the Word of God refers specifically to a place, a person, an amount, or a number of any kind, that there is significance to that name or number. Mark 8:22 opens with a very important phrase, "And he cometh to Bethsaida." Bethsaida was a beautiful seaport city, somewhat prosperous in that day. It was about one hundred miles north/northeast of Jerusalem on the northeast shore of the Sea of Galilee near where the Jordan River empties into the Sea of Galilee. About two miles directly to the west of Bethsaida was a city called Capernaum. Both of these cities were renowned in the earthly ministry of Jesus, and He performed a number of miracles in these cities.

The first recorded visit of Jesus to Bethsaida occurred during the first year of His earthly ministry. It was on this visit that Jesus called Philip to follow Him. Philip, Andrew, and Peter were all from Bethsaida, and Peter also had a home in nearby Capernaum.

Jesus' second recorded visit to Bethsaida occurred during the second year of His earthly ministry. While He was there, He spoke to the city and sharply rebuked its people. He rebuked them because, in spite of the fact that they had witnessed and experienced many great miracles, they had not repented. Matthew 11:21-22 states that Jesus said, "Woe unto thee, Chorazin! Woe unto thee, Bethsaida! For if the mighty works, which were done in you, had been done in Tyre and Sidon, they would have repented long ago in sackcloth and ashes. But I say unto you, It shall be more tolerable for Tyre and Sidon at the day of judgment than for you." That was obviously a very stern, sobering, and serious rebuke.

There is no further record of Jesus being in Bethsaida until the third year of His earthly ministry. Shortly after John the Baptist was beheaded, Jesus sent His disciples out two by two and anointed them to do the work of the ministry. They returned with testimonies of great ministry and miracles. Then Jesus took His disciples to a desert place belonging to Bethsaida to rest for awhile. While they were there, people in surrounding cities heard that Jesus was there and they flocked to Him. He taught them, and it was in that desert place belonging to Bethsaida that He fed the five thousand men plus women and children. There is only one other record of Jesus going to Bethsaida, and it was in His third year of ministry. During a trip through Galilee, He went to Bethsaida, where He healed the blind man, which is the miracle we are studying (Mark 8:22-26).

God's Heart to Return

It's comforting to know that Jesus would return to a city even after He had sharply rebuked it for its sins, but that's the kind of God we serve! He never disqualifies, dismisses or turns His back on us. Jesus displayed this kind of love when He traveled to Gadara to minister to the demon possessed man in the Gadarenes, as recorded in Mark 5:1-20. Gad was one of the tribes of Israel, along with Reuben and half of the tribe of Manasseh, that didn't settle in the Promised Land. The tribe of Gad crossed over the Jordan and fought alongside the other tribes to take the Promised Land, but then Gad crossed back over the Jordan and settled on the other side. The Gadarenes could have been living in the Promised Land but they had chosen not to do so, in effect rejecting what God desired for them. However, Jesus showed them that God still loved them by going back to Gadara to deliver the demon possessed man. I'm so glad we serve that kind of God!

What had happened to the people in Bethsaida that they became hardened to miracles? Had they seen so many miracles that they had become jaded? Had they become hardened to the Word because they had heard it so often, and they were no longer stirred or blessed by it? Their hearts had grown cold, but God still loved them and proved it, because Jesus went back to Bethsaida!

Telling Jesus What to Do

When Jesus came to Bethsaida, they brought a blind man to him. I'm glad for "they." I don't know who "they" were but I'm glad they had enough wisdom to bring the blind man to Jesus and not to the Pharisees, the Sadducees, or the chief priests. They brought the blind man to the right place and more specifically to the right Person.

The blind man was living in a much different world than sighted people. His world was a world of darkness. He could not see and could only imagine. His world could be a world of confusion, because he couldn't follow signs and had no direction. In the natural, perhaps of all of the senses we possess, the most serious one to lose is the eyesight. A blind person has to be led around by others. Someone has to tell them where to go and where they are. The latter part of Mark 8:22 declares, "They said to Jesus, touch him." Isn't it interesting how many times we come to Jesus and tell Him what we think He should do? These people at Bethsaida thought they already knew the solution and what Jesus needed to do..."Jesus, just touch him and he will be okay, then he can go on living." It's kind of like giving him a band aid and saying, "Just fix it Jesus!"

When my oldest son was very young he thought that his Dad could do anything, and he had a tendency to break his toys. He would come to me with his hands full of parts and pieces and say, "Daddy, fix it," so I become the fixer. I see a similar characteristic or mindset in these people at Bethsaida. "Jesus, touch him and he's going to be alright. He's going to be able to make it in life. He's going to know what to do. Touch him Jesus. We've watched You and we know You're able to touch him." Sometimes, we go to Jesus in crisis situations and say, "I have a problem, and I need a solution. I have a question, and I need an answer. I have a need that must be met." There is nothing unscriptural about realizing that He is our provider, healer, and helper. However, I see a narrowness, a shallowness, and a kind of human focus here, because God is bigger than all that.

A Journey, Not an Experience

The next verse (Mark 8:23) doesn't say that Jesus *touched* him. It says Jesus *took* him by the hand. Please note that this blind man, in order to take Jesus' hand, had to drop the hands of others. Jesus did not simply want to give this man an experience. He wanted to take him on a life-changing journey, because He led him out of the city. Jesus was essentially saying, "If you're going to identify with Me, we're going somewhere. Are you willing to go? Are you willing to take a tight grip on My hand? Do you believe Me? Do you trust Me? We're on a journey." Jesus led him out of the city, a city that was renowned for not repenting.

It is very vital in our relationship with the Lord to understand the importance of repentance. Jesus didn't rebuke the city because it had done things wrong, made mistakes, or simply because it had sinned. He rebuked it because the people didn't repent of what they did. He was effectively saying to the blind man, "I am going to take you out of the place of unrepentance." It is interesting that after Jesus healed the man, He effectively told him, "Don't ever go back there again. Don't go back to what I took you out of. "

Jesus had him by the hand. The men who had brought him to Jesus may have thought, "He's not answering our prayer. We told Jesus to touch him and He's not touching him." There was never a question of whether this man was going to be healed. His eyes were going to be opened. When we come to Jesus, He will take care of whatever we need. Sometimes, though, we put the cart before the horse. The deeper issue was not whether the man would be healed. The issue was that Jesus was taking him somewhere, on a journey, and in the process he was going to be healed. If Jesus would have only touched him and released him, he would have been a man that could see in a city of unrepentance. Jesus' plan for him was greater than that. I am so thankful that God's plan doesn't end with the born-again experience. The experience is only the beginning for us, because He has something greater in mind for us. Jesus had something greater in mind for this blind man as well, so He took him by the hand and led him out of the city.

Taking Away the Curse

After He had taken him out of the village, Jesus spit on his eyes and He put His hands of him. Please note the conjunction "and" in this sequence. Jesus both spit on his eyes _and_ put His hands on him. When we put this all together, we can see the deeper truths that the Holy Spirit is showing us through this healing. At this point in the story, Jesus now has this man wholly submitted to Him. Jesus has taken his hand. The man has let go his friends and has walked out of the place of unrepentance with Jesus, and now Jesus is beginning to minister to him. Jesus spits on him. To us, it doesn't sound like the cleanest or holiest way to heal a blind man. For a moment, the man may have been uncertain of whether Jesus was for him or against him, because spittle is a type of the curse, and when someone spits on another, it can be symbolic of transferring the curse.

In Jewish custom, when a young girl was caught in immorality, she would be taken to the town square where the elders would gather. The father of the family would come and spit on her, symbolizing transference of the curse of the family on her. Did you ever realize the significance that Jesus was spit upon during His trial? It was extremely significant because it signified that He took our curse upon Himself. Collectively, as sinners, we spit on Him and transferred the curse to Him. This account of the blind man would be difficult to understand if it ended with the spitting, but the word "and" follows immediately! Symbolically, with the spitting, the man became a victim of the curse, but then Jesus immediately took His hands, I believe, and wiped the man's eyes. Jesus wiped the curse off of him. Jesus put His hands on the man and wiped his eyes, signifying He was taking away the curse.

Trees Walking

Jesus then asked the man if he saw anything. Upon Jesus' touch, the man immediately was transported out of a world of darkness into a world of light. This is a type of when we are born-again, when He removes the curse and transfers us out of darkness and into light. Jesus said, "Do you see anything?" The man replied, "Yes, I see men as trees walking." I am glad at that point in the journey that the man didn't get so excited about going from darkness to light that he ran away to live his own life.

If the man had given his testimony at that point, he would have been speaking heresy. I can see the title of his first sermon: "Trees walk." That's all he said, "Trees walk." Heresy enters in when we start saying what we think we see. On the morning of Jesus' resurrection, the women that ran to the empty tomb went back and told the disciples that someone had stolen Jesus' body because they saw the stone rolled away. They didn't get close enough to see a complete picture, so they preached heresy. They only saw in part. Peter and

John took off running toward the tomb to see for themselves. John outran Peter and, arriving at the tomb first, he looked in and saw the grave clothes. When Peter arrived, he wasn't satisfied simply looking into the tomb, and he went in and saw the napkin folded neatly. Peter knew that no one had gotten to Jesus....He had gotten to them! Peter saw clearly, and knew that Jesus had indeed arisen from the dead!

As we grow closer to the Lord in our walk with Him, we begin to understand the full message and see more clearly. Of course trees don't walk, but this was part of the blind man's journey, part of the process. Likewise, we don't see things clearly right away. Unfortunately, sometimes when a person is born again and has a zeal to preach, they are placed in pulpits before they are truly ready for the responsibility of preaching the complete message of the Gospel. It takes training and time to mature in ministry. People need to sit under, and be mentored by, experienced pastors in order to prepare them for the work ahead. We often think when we go from darkness to light that we see it all right away. No, we see differently but not clearly. There's a difference between *differently* and *clearly*. This blind man did the right thing when he first went from darkness to light because he stayed near Jesus. He submitted Himself to the growth and healing process through which Jesus was taking him, and Jesus touched him again.

Look Up!

Why did Jesus touch him twice? It was not because Jesus was having a bad day, wasn't prayed up, or didn't have enough power or anointing. Jesus could have healed the man with one touch, one look, or one word, but the journey was more important than the experience. When Jesus touched the man the second time, the Bible says that the man was restored, and then Jesus made the man look up. The Greek word translated "restored" is *apokatastasis* which means "to be reconstituted, to be brought back to the original like you once were." It means more than simply being healed. It refers to being <u>whole</u>.

Jesus made the man look up. It isn't a natural human tendency to look up. We tend to look down in shame, look back at our past, or perhaps look around at people. Sometimes we look around until we find someone that's so bad that they make us look good, but *God is teaching us to look up*. Psalm 121:1-2 declares, "I will lift up mine eyes unto the hills from whence cometh my help. My help cometh from the Lord which made heaven and earth." Hebrews 12:2 states, "Looking unto Jesus the author and finisher of our faith; who for the joy that was set before him endured the cross, despising the shame, and is set down at the right hand of the throne of God." Jesus told the man to look up, and when he did, what did he see? He saw Jesus of course. The man looked up, saw the Word of God, and said that he saw all things clearly. He saw all things clearly, which means he saw them as Jesus saw them. Jesus sees everything clearly.

At this point, I believe the man had moved from the realm of seeing men as trees to the realm of seeing people as people. Trees are inanimate objects which are used to make other things for our purposes. We cut trees up, plane them, drill them, saw them, and sand them. If we see people as things or objects, we can never be used as God desires, because we will think that people are simply to be used for our purposes. We may try to simply use people to help us or bless us, but that is not the way God sees people nor wants them to be treated!

Seeing People as Jesus Sees Them

The Word of God teaches us how Jesus sees people, and on more than one occasion the Bible states He looked upon them and had compassion on them. Luke 19:41 declares that Jesus wept over Jerusalem. Matthew 9:36 states that He was moved with compassion for them because they were like sheep that had no shepherd. Jesus sees people as hurting, confused, needy, broken, discouraged, and disappointed, and He is moved with compassion to minister to all.

We are living in a generation of broken, dysfunctional people and, except for the grace of God, we are all in the same condition. Someone said to me once, "I have never met a family that wasn't dysfunctional to some extent." I believe that an extremely important part of the effectiveness of the ministry of Jesus was what He saw when He looked at someone. He saw brokenness, and when He did, He would heal it. That's why people ran to Jesus. They would come and press upon Him because they knew that He saw what other people didn't see. They knew that if they could get close to Him, they would walk away differently than when they came.

I firmly believe that we're on the threshold of a great harvest and a great move of God, and I believe it will come through the people of God. We must move away from thinking that only pastors and evangelists are going to bring in the harvest. We are all intended to be involved in God's work! God has placed His call and anointing on every believer. I believe God is going to cause us, wherever He has placed us in our job, school, or community, to hear the cry of the hurting and see the plight of the needy. We will know that it is only the love of Jesus, the mercy and grace of God, that will turn them around and make them whole. The blind man was no longer blind. He saw clearly!

Jesus had taken the man out of the city (Bethsaida) known for its unrepentance. The man was now healed, and Jesus was effectively saying, "You must live in a state of repentance." When we try to go on the journey without walking in repentance, it will hinder our relationship with God as well as our ministry. Jesus took him out of there and effectively said, "I never want you to go back there again. Don't go back there even though you feel so much better than you felt before your encounter with Me. Live a life of being at My feet and being on your face before Me." That day, the man moved from more than darkness to light. He moved to the place of seeing with spiritual eyes as God sees.

God's Power for Our Generation

It always blesses me that whenever Jesus called anything out, He always healed it. He didn't expose people and then leave them in their condition. He always healed them. The power to heal, make whole, restore, change, and lift up is the anointing of the Holy Spirit that comes upon His people and His church to bring in the harvest. We could look at our generation and conclude there has never been a generation as bad as this one, but if we do that, we are "looking at trees." The alternative is to look at this generation and understand that there has never been an opportunity like we have today. When we do that, we are seeing clearly. People do some of the bad things they do because they are hurting, confused, and needy. I once heard the phrase, "Hurting people hurt people" and I believe it to be true. People that hurt others are often people that have been hurt themselves and don't know how to process their pain. Lord Jesus, help us. Touch us again. Touch our eyes so we can see the hurting and bring Your healing and wholeness to them!

I see in this miracle a great manifestation of the power of God, but I also see the transformation of a man who was willing to go with Jesus all the way, willing to hang onto His hand even though He didn't know where they were going or what was happening. Somewhere along that journey the man was spit upon, but it was wiped off. Somewhere along that journey Jesus made him look up, and it began a new life for him.

My prayer is that God will touch all of our eyes and heal us so we can be healers, that He will change us so we can be restorers, and that He will use us so He can be glorified. I believe that is His heart's desire. Our generation is filled with frailties, faults, weaknesses, imperfections, blemishes, defects, hurts, pains, loneliness, and confusion, but Jesus is here to bring healing. I pray that as we get close to Jesus, we will see the greatest victories and the greatest manifestation of the power of God we have ever seen. It's going to come through us, because each of us has a sphere of influence, a certain number of people we touch that perhaps no one else will touch.   There are people watching how we live our lives, and wondering if we care, if God cares, and if their situation can be turned around. Lord, help us, anoint us, and touch us again. Touch our eyes again, Jesus. We don't want to see trees walking, we want to see the hearts of hurting people that you want to heal. We want to see You take people from blindness to clear sight!

Born to Carry the King

John 18:37 records the account of Pilate asking Jesus, "Art thou a king then?" and Jesus responding by declaring, "Thou sayest that I am a king. To this end was I born, and for this cause came I into the world, that I should bear witness unto the truth." I'm convinced that one of the reasons the earthly ministry of Jesus Christ was so effective was that He knew His purpose. He knew that He was born for a reason. He came for a purpose and He never deviated from that purpose. He kept His eyes on it throughout His time upon this earth. God has created each of us for a purpose, and as we understand our purpose, I believe we come into a dimension of fulfillment and satisfaction that nothing else in this world can bring. Our innermost being is satisfied when we walk in the purpose for which we were created. We may be called to different offices, different responsibilities and different locations. We may be called to different paths in life but we all have a purpose.

The Triumphal Entry

The triumphal entry of Jesus into Jerusalem occurred five days before Calvary. It is one of the few events that were recorded by all four gospel writers. Mark's account contains some specific details which I believe are important to what God is speaking to us today. Mark 11:1-8 declares, "And when they came nigh to Jerusalem, unto Bethphage and Bethany, at the mount of Olives, he sendeth forth two of his disciples. And saith unto them, Go your way into the village over against you; and as soon as ye be entered into it, ye shall find a colt tied, whereon never man sat; loose him, and bring him. And if any man say unto you, Why do ye this? Say ye that the Lord hath need of him; and straightway he will send him hither. And they went their way, and found the colt tied by the door without in a place where two ways met;

and they loose him. And certain of them that stood there said unto them, What do ye, loosing the colt? And they said unto them even as Jesus had commanded; and they let them go. And they brought the colt to Jesus, and cast their garments on him; and he sat upon him. And many spread their garments in the way; and others cut down branches off the trees, and strawed them in the way."

That must have been a glorious, magnificent event to witness. I can imagine the excitement and joy that surrounded the occasion as Jesus entered Jerusalem to be presented as king. Many people followed Him crying, "Hosanna! Blessed is He who comes in the name of the Lord!" They were waving palm branches and laying their garments down before Him. They were excitedly exalting the King of Kings.

The Little Donkey

God spoke through the prophet Zechariah five hundred years before this event, and the prophesy refers to a significant part of this story that we tend to overlook or regard lightly. Zechariah 9:9 declares, "Rejoice greatly, o daughter of Zion; shout, O daughter of Jerusalem; behold thy king cometh unto thee; he is just and having salvation; lowly, and riding upon an ass, and upon a colt the foal of an ass."

Zechariah's prophecy, as well as the accounts of Matthew, Mark, Luke, and John, not only speak of the glory of the event, but also the animal upon which Jesus made His entry into Jerusalem, the means by which God declared the glory of His Son as the king. Matthew and Luke wrote that Jesus entered Jerusalem on a colt. Mark, like Zechariah, wrote that he came on an ass, a colt, the foal of an ass. John wrote that He came on an ass's colt. It seems important to the Holy Spirit as He communicates the Word of God to us that we understand the means by which Jesus was presented as king in that day to that generation. God had planned from the foundation of the world that Jesus would be presented as king on a colt, the foal of an ass. The word *foal* refers to a very young colt who is less than one year old. The word *colt* refers to a foolish, unmanageable thing. As I studied this, I asked the Lord about the significance of the colt and how it applies to us in our day. One day as I was reading the Bible, I came across Job

11:12, which states, "....though man be born like a wild ass's colt."

I then began to understand that what happened on the day of Jesus' triumphal entry was a prophetic type of what God wants to do through us in this day. That little donkey was a very special little donkey because he was both created by Jesus and chosen by Him. He was simply a little donkey who carried the king into Jerusalem and then isn't mentioned after that in the Bible. We don't know much about the donkey. We don't know the color of his hair or his eyes. All we know is that he was just a young little colt, a young little donkey.

The Lord chose the donkey and gave him a destiny, which was to carry the King. He was a donkey with a destiny! In Job 11:12, God equates that donkey to mankind, and therefore the donkey is a prophetic type of what God has called us to be and to do. In the same way that He created that donkey to carry Jesus into Jerusalem, He has created us to carry the king to our generation, not on our backs but in our hearts. Therefore, in seeing us, the world will see the king. In touching us, the world will touch the king, and in crossing our paths the world will be confronted with the king. We are effectively "donkeys with a destiny." We have been created by God with the God ordained purpose of carrying the king to our generation.

Redeemed!

There are parallels between the day that little donkey carried Jesus, and our day in which we are to carry Jesus. First of all, the donkey was a _redeemed_ donkey. As part of the Old Testament law, Exodus 13:13 declares, "And every firstling of an ass thou shalt redeem with a lamb; and if thou wilt not redeem it, then thou shalt break his neck." That sounds very strange until we begin to see that this is a Biblical type and foreshadow of Jesus redeeming mankind. The owner had to choose between killing the newborn donkey or killing a lamb to allow the donkey to live.

The donkey that carried Jesus was definitely a redeemed donkey since he was obviously alive, which means that at some point a lamb had died for that donkey. Think about the choice that the donkey's owner had before him. As soon as that little firstling was born and the owner looked at that little slobbering mess, he had to make a decision to either kill a lamb so that the donkey could live or break the donkey's neck. The owner didn't make his decision based on the way the donkey appeared at that time. Instead, the owner would think about the future. Someday the donkey would carry his burden. Someday the donkey would pull the wagon to bring in the harvest. Because the donkey had been born for a purpose, the owner slayed a lamb to allow the donkey to live.

Likewise, God the Father looked ahead to the time we would be born in our trespasses and sins, the messy product of the seed of Adam. However, God overlooked our condition and saw our potential. God thought of each of us and said, "They are worth my best Lamb." On the day when Father led the Lamb to the cross, He was thinking about us and the day when we could carry the King of Kings and help bring in His harvest. The devil may try to tell us that we are worthless, that we have messed up so badly that there is no hope. The devil is a liar! God loves all of us and Jesus died for us because He saw in each of us a little donkey that could carry the king to this generation.

The Commonness of the Donkey

When I think about Father choosing a donkey to carry the King, I am struck with the fact that is is such a common animal. If I were running the kingdom and I was going to send the king into Jerusalem, I would prepare a group of stallions pulling a gold plated chariot. He's certainly worthy of that. However, the Father chose a donkey, a colt...a foolish, unmanageable thing. Paul wrote to the church at Corinth, as recorded in I Corinthians 1:27, "But God hath chosen the foolish things of the world to confound the wise; and God hath chosen the weak things of the world to confound the things which are mighty; And base things of the world that no flesh should glory in his presence." God has chosen things which are considered worthless by many. He effectively says, "I'd rather have donkeys. Horses are beautiful and camels are impressive, but I've chosen little foolish, unmanageable things." Such were some of us. None of us were accidents when we were born. The purpose always comes before the person. There was a purpose for each of us before we were born. The devil might say, "You're nothing but a little old donkey, smelly and weak" but we can reply, "But I'm carrying the king!"

God Includes Us in His Miracles

Please note that Jesus didn't instruct the disciples to simply find any donkey. He told them to go and find a specific donkey. We are individually chosen by God for His purposes. Jesus told the disciples to get that specific donkey, and when people asked them why they were untying him, they were to say that the Lord needed that donkey. That staggers my mind. God is the self-sufficient, self-sustaining one of all ages. He didn't need the donkey out of lack because God doesn't lack anything. God "chose to need" the donkey, and us, out of love so that He could provide us the opportunity to be a part of the miracle that He is going to perform.

None of us can win a soul. It takes the Holy Spirit to bring someone to Jesus. I've become more conscious of this in my years of preaching. It's not my preaching. I simply talk about Jesus. When God called me as a boy, I told the Lord that I didn't have an unusual, powerful, miraculous testimony that would bring people to hear me preach. I don't mean to trivialize that, because I thank God for miraculous testimonies, but I didn't have one. I wasn't delivered out of a life of crime or addiction. I said, "God, nobody's going to listen to me. Who wants to hear me?" I felt that God spoke to me clearly and said, "Then you're going to have to talk about Me." The central theme of my message all my life has been *Jesus, Jesus, Jesus*. He chooses to need us. Isn't that wonderful of Him?

Lazarus had been dead four days, and Jesus stood at the grave and said, "Lazarus come forth". Lazarus came out, bound hand and foot in grave clothes. If Jesus had enough power to raise Lazarus from the dead, after his body had already started to decompose, surely He had enough power to bring Lazarus out of the grave unwrapped! Of course He did. It wasn't due to a lack of power; it was because Jesus wanted to let His disciples participate in the miracle. He effectively said, "I'm going to let you be a part of what I'm doing. I'm going to let you be a part of what Father has called Me to do today. You unwrap him."

John 21:1-14 records the account of when some of the disciples became discouraged and, at Peter's request, they went fishing. They fished all night on the Sea of Galilee and caught nothing. To add insult to injury, a man called from the shore (they didn't yet realize it was Jesus) and asked them how they were doing. They replied that they had caught nothing. Jesus then told them cast the net on the right side of the boat. These men were fisherman by trade and likely proud of their fishing ability. They spent the whole night and had caught nothing, but they obeyed His Word and the fish came swimming into the net and filled it up. Jesus had allowed them to be successful. He had filled the net with fish. Note that Jesus didn't need those fish, because He was already cooking fish on a fire, but He wanted to include them in the working of this great miracle.

The Donkey's Problems

When Jesus was instructing the disciples to get the donkey, He told them to say that the Lord needs this donkey. He was effectively saying, "I have caused him to be born. I have caused a lamb to die so that he can live, and I have chosen to ride into Jerusalem on this donkey." We are blessed as His people because we have been chosen to carry the king. This donkey has been birthed and a lamb has died so it could live. Jesus has chosen the donkey, but I see that the donkey still had four problems, four issues.

The first problem was that he was tied. Men had tied him to a post. The donkey had more potential than he was presently experiencing. He had been born to carry the king but he was tied to the post. Jesus instructed His disciples to untie him. In our lives, we can become tied up by actions, thoughts, circumstances, and lies the devil tells us which inhibit, limit, and restrain us from being everything that God has created us to be. Jesus not only chose the donkey, but He told the disciples to untie him.

The second problem was that this was a donkey that no man had ever ridden. We would call that an unbroken donkey, and we could liken it to someone with an independent spirit. We sometimes think, "I'll do it my way" and we don't want to be told what to do. However, there has never been a donkey that Jesus couldn't ride. Some of us had that kind of unbroken, independent spirit before Jesus got hold of our heart. Jesus takes care of the independent spirit that originally got mankind in trouble way back in the Garden of Eden. He never gives up on anyone, regardless of how independent they may be. Likewise, we also must never give up on anyone that seems too independent or headstrong to come to Jesus. We must not give up, but instead we must intercede, pray, and believe. There has never been a donkey Jesus can't ride. God often calls the people that we thought would never submit to Him, the ones that no one has been able to ride. God says, "That's the one I want. Go get him."

The third problem was that the donkey was at a fork in the road. Jesus described the donkey as being at a place where two roads meet. Jesus didn't want them simply to loose the donkey, because he could have taken the wrong route. Jesus wanted them to hold the rope and lead the donkey all the way to Him. With every step they took, they were one step closer to Jesus, and they had the donkey on the right road. This speaks to me of discipleship. We must not only help people to be loosed from their bondage, but we must also do all we can to disciple them, walking alongside them, bringing them closer and closer to Jesus.

The fourth problem was that the donkey was barebacked. The Bible says that when the disciples got the donkey to Jesus, they put their garments on him and then Jesus sat upon him. Why did Jesus not sit on that donkey until the garments were on the donkey's back? I believe it is because the Lord will never ride on flesh. Flesh must be covered over. Romans 8:7 declares that our flesh is at enmity with God. Flesh cannot please God, and in fact it is repulsive to Him. We used to sing a song whose lyrics said, "I'm covered over with a robe of righteousness that Jesus gave to me." In order to carry the king, we must apply the blood of Jesus that covers us, remits our sin, and cleanses us from all unrighteousness. We must be covered, then we're ready to carry the king.

Carrying the King

That little donkey could have thought, "This is really living. All of these people are laying down their garments and I get to walk on them. They are waving palm branches and shouting 'Hosanna!'" However, the donkey must have realized that they were not cheering for him, but rather for the one that he was carrying. We must never forget that as God uses us, all glory and honor and praise belongs to the one we are carrying. We were born to carry the king, and as soon as we finish our task, we will disappear off the pages of life. Our mission will be accomplished and our job will be done.

The apostle Paul put it this way in II Timothy 4:7, which states, "I have finished my course." Paul was saying, "I have carried the king to my generation." Paul had himself been an unbroken donkey before Jesus met him on the road to Damascus. The Bible doesn't specifically say whether he was walking or riding, but there was a good chance that he was riding on his own donkey and Jesus had to knock him off that so that he would become the donkey on whom Jesus would ride.

We must all ask God whether we are walking out and living out the purpose for which we were born. We must never let the devil tell us that we are not useful to God. There are many people that have never stood behind a pulpit or sang into a microphone that have carried the king to their generation in marvelous ways. It doesn't matter if anyone knows our name or not. We don't know the name of that donkey either. It doesn't matter if anyone feels that we are attractive because we don't know the color of the eyes of that donkey either. The one thing we do know is that the donkey was created for a purpose and a lamb died so that he could fulfill it.

I pray for you today if you find yourself tied to a post. Perhaps the devil has tried to make you think that your past mistakes have caused you to miss out on the opportunity to be what you were created to be. The devil is a liar, but God loves you. You've been both born and called for a purpose. Today is the day to get untied from whatever has bound you. If you have had unforgiveness in your heart, release it and lay it down at the feet of Jesus. You have a higher calling than to carry that burden. You don't have to walk under the load of your past, your failures, and your weaknesses. You're not just a donkey. You're _that_ donkey. You were born to carry the king!

Can These Bones Live?

About six hundred years before the earthly ministry of Christ, the Word of God and secular history both confirm that Israel was in one of the worst, most deplorable conditions of its entire history. They had found themselves in difficult places many times before, but this situation was thought by many to be the worst of the worst. It was so bad that many people had given up any hope that they would ever be a nation or ever have a future again.

Babylon had come down, swept through Jerusalem, and torn down the walls of the city. They ransacked the temple and took all of the precious vessels that were so sacred to the Israelites. Not only was Jerusalem left in total ruin, but the Babylonians also carried off over 70,000 men, women and children to Babylon as captives, without promise of ever returning again. They spent years longing for their freedom, hoping to return to Jerusalem, but as time progressed, it became more clear that there was no desire in the hearts of the Babylonians to let them go. In Babylon, the Israelite captives wallowed in the memories of everything that was precious to them that had been torn from them, and they struggled to keep hope alive.

The Hand of the Lord

One of the captives was a young man in his twenties named Ezekiel who was living by the River Chebar when the Spirit of the Lord began to give him a series of visions. One of the visions God gave him is recorded in the thirty-seventh chapter of the Book of Ezekiel. This is possibly one of the most popular chapters of one of the most popular prophetic books in the Old Testament. The vision is recorded beginning with Ezekiel 37:1, which states, "The hand of the Lord was upon me, and carried me out in the spirit of the Lord."

When the hand of the Lord comes upon our lives, the Holy Spirit begins to transport us and direct our lives. Once we're touched by God, we'll never be the same again. Our agenda, our goals, and our daily walk through life will change in dramatic ways. The hand of the Lord upon someone's life makes all the difference in the world. Despite the dire situation in which His people found themselves in Ezekiel's day, God hadn't given up on Israel. God will never give up on His people and He will never give up on you or me.

God loves each and every one of us, and once He touches us, we can be certain that His direction for our lives are set. In fact, He knew what He wanted our lives to be even before He created us. God knows the end from the beginning. He often intervenes in situations such as Israel's that are dark, dismal, and hopeless. When the Bible uses the phrase "But God..." we can be certain that it is referring to divine intervention in the lives of men. Many of us have had "But God..." experiences in our lives. Perhaps we didn't recognize it at the time. Perhaps we were in a situation where we didn't know what to do, we had a question we couldn't answer, a mountain we couldn't climb, or a river we couldn't cross. We couldn't see our next step or know where our provision would come from.....but God intervened and showed His mighty hand. Likewise, in Israel's desperate situation, God in His sovereignty decided to put His hand on Ezekiel to direct him and lead him.

Note that in Ezekiel 37:1, as a result of the Spirit of the Lord placing His hand on Ezekiel, He transported him. Ezekiel, by the River Chebar, suddenly found himself transported in this vision by the Spirit of the Lord, and set down in a valley of bones. Many times, when the hand of the Lord is upon us, guiding our lives, we suddenly find ourselves in a place where we look around and wonder how we got there. We wonder what set of circumstances caused us to make this decision, take that direction, or choose that path that led us to this place. The only real answer to those questions is that it was the sovereign hand of the Spirit of the Lord.

The Valley of Dry Bones

Ezekiel found himself transported by the Spirit to a valley of bones. As Ezekiel was explaining the vision, it was becoming clearer to him, and he was becoming more focused on the message that God was giving him. Ezekiel 37:2 declares, "And caused me." Ezekiel realized that the Spirit of the Lord "caused" him to do something. The Hebrew word translated "caused" is *nawthan* which literally means He *directed* or *charged* Ezekiel. The use of this word indicates that Ezekiel felt that what God was showing him was an essential part of his life, and that he felt it was absolutely essential to take the next step because he knew God had charged him. What did God charge him to do? God charged him "....to pass by them (the bones) round about."

God didn't place Ezekiel on a ledge or a high mountain where he could look down into the valley and see bones scattered all over. The Spirit of the Lord did not simply *show* him the valley, but placed him *in* the valley and caused him to walk *among* the bones in the valley. Ezekiel walked among the bones and was therefore able to observe their condition close up. During an autopsy, when a body is in an advanced state of decay, the examiner can make a determination regarding the cause of death based on the condition of the bones. Bones show evidence of fracture, bruising, or crushing. Bones tell a story and speak a message, and God caused Ezekiel to walk among them, step between them, and step over them. He wanted Ezekiel to see the condition of the bones in this valley and Ezekiel made two observations. First, he said there are <u>many</u> bones. He used the word many, which we can conclude was another way of saying enumerable. Secondly, he described the bones as being very <u>dry</u>, which indicates that all evidence of life had escaped.

God's Question

In Ezekiel's vision, God's hand was upon him and the Spirit had transported him to the valley of dry bones, into the midst of an overwhelmingly gloomy scene that appeared to have no hope. It seemed that there was no possibility the bones would ever live again. Then, God asked Ezekiel a very interesting question, recorded in Ezekiel 37:3a, "And he said unto me, Son of man, can these bones live?"

God never asks a question to obtain information. He wasn't trying to gain enough information from Ezekiel to make a decision in order to know what to do. One of God's attributes is omniscience, which means He knows everything about all things, all the time, everywhere. God, who is all knowing, asked a question. Why did He ask a question?

Jesus also asked questions during His earthly ministry. At the Pool of Bethesda, Jesus looked at a man that had been lame for thirty-eight years and asked, "Do you want to be whole?" If one wasn't aware that God has perfect wisdom, they could almost think that was a foolish question. However, when God asks a question, He does it for our (the hearer's) sake. He does it so we can see what is in our own hearts. Luke 6:45 declares, "Out of the abundance of the heart the mouth speaketh." When God asks a question, it's like holding a mirror in front of us and asking us to look at ourselves. What comes out of our mouth is an indication of what's in our heart, and it is often a surprise to even us. Most of us have heard something come out of our mouth that we didn't know was in our heart. Many times God must put that mirror in front of us because He's about to do another great work in us, but we can't go to the next level until we see where we currently are.

When we examine the dialogue between Jesus and the lame man at the Pool of Bethesda, we will find this principle in evidence, because the man's answer revealed the condition of his heart. The man effectively said, "I have two problems, Jesus. The first is that every time the water is stirred I don't have anyone to take me to the water." In other words he was saying, "It is their fault." He was blaming his condition on others, using the familiar excuse that it is always someone else's fault. Obviously the man's condition was not someone else's fault because if that was the case, Jesus could have assigned one of his disciples to stay there and help the man into the water. The second thing the man said to Jesus was, effectively, "Someone always gets there before I do." He was basically saying, "It is not fair."   The man's response revealed that he wasn't taking any initiative for himself, but instead he was lamenting his condition as a victim. Our answers to God's questions reveal the human heart!

Ezekiel's Answer

God asked Ezekiel, "Can these bones live?" What would

Ezekiel's answer be, since he had just observed how numerous and how dry the bones were? There was no evidence of life nor apparent possibility that they could ever live, yet God was asking him if they could live. How would we answer that question? Perhaps we would say something to the effect of "Yes God, they can, because I don't want to tell You that You can't do something."

The name Ezekiel literally means "God is strong." With a name like that, it seems it would constrain him to say, "Certainly they can live." There is nothing that God can't do, because the Hebrew word translated "strong" means He is mentally, intellectually, physically and morally superior to any other being. However, Ezekiel had just walked through the bones, stepping over them and seeing up close how dry they were. His natural mind must have been thinking, "It's impossible. It's too late. This situation can't possibly change. There's no way this can turn around."

Ezekiel must have had a raging internal conflict. The Spirit of the Lord puts him in a bone yard. Ezekiel examines, analyzes, and touches the bones, and God comes to him with this question. Ezekiel sees their dire condition, yet he has a name that says "God is strong," that He is superior physically, morally, and intellectually to any other being. God is above all. Ezekiel's answer is found in Ezekiel 37:3b, which states, "And I answered, O Lord God, thou knowest." He may have been thinking, "Lord, I'm conflicted. Everything that makes sense to me says 'No, these bones cannot live' and yet I've been given a name that declares that the very one that's asking the question has more power than any other force in the entire universe."

Triage

In the medical field, the word _triage_ means to define a system of assessing the severity of the injured and prioritizing each one's treatment to insure the greatest number of survivors. For example, in a disaster situation, there may be hundreds or thousands of people in need, but a limited number of nurses, doctors, and medicine. First responders arrive and make a quick assessment of the situation. They check the vital signs of individuals. They visually check their condition.

They make a determination as to the state that each patient is in, and they have four kinds of tags that they put on the patients. If a person only has minor injuries such as scratches or superficial bruises, they put a green tag on them. If they have deeper wounds or more serious issues such as broken bones, they put a yellow tag on them. If the injured person is in a very dire situation, they put a red tag on them.

However, when they encounter someone that either appears to be dead or in such bad condition that there is little or no hope they will survive, they call these people unsalvageable or discards, and they put a black tag on them. After the initial evaluation, they take the people with the green and yellow tags and set them aside for a while because they can last a while without treatment. The people with red tags are rushed immediately to hospitals or medical facilities so they can be treated immediately in an effort to save their life. However, they put a black tag on the "discards" and send them to the morgue, even though some of them may even have life left in them. The medical personnel know that there is no way with the limited amount of resources available that they can spend the time and resources on that person because it would mean they will lose others that are salvageable.

Black Tags

I know that process sounds a bit inhuman, but this is literally what happens. Triage creates an interesting situation because humanity is admitting that there are conditions beyond repair, beyond salvaging. However, the church of Jesus Christ should never pass out black tags. We believe in prayer, and we believe in a God that is able to do all things!

In the earthly ministry of Jesus, He never walked around passing out black tags. In fact, He removed them! One day, He encountered a funeral procession near Nain and among the mourners was a mother who was weeping. She was a widow, and now she lost her son as well. Jesus had compassion on her, and He went over and took the black tag off her son and He said, "Get up!"

One day, word came to Jesus that his close friend Lazarus was gravely ill, and the messenger's implication was that Jesus had better get there right away. However, Jesus was moved by the Father's direction and not by emotional pleas. Four days later He arrived in Bethany and Mary and Martha effectively said, "Oh Jesus, if you would have only arrived when our brother Lazarus had the red tag on... but we're so sorry, because he's black tagged now." Jesus effectively responded, "Roll away the stone, I'm collecting black tags today!"

Jesus also took the black tag off of Jairus' daughter. Then, there was the madman in Gadara who was cutting himself and was living among the tombs, and Jesus took his black tag off. I am so glad that we serve a God that has that kind of anointing and power! He has the name that is above every name, and at the mention of that name, every knee shall bow and every tongue shall confess. God has given you and I that name, and He has commissioned us not to put black tags on anyone. We must do everything within our power to take black tags off! There is no person that is "unsalvageable" in the mind of God. Jesus was drawn to the diseased, the forgotten, the hungry, the ostracized, and the poor. Jesus went around and He ministered life. He removed black tags!

Messing Up the Bone Yard

The Spirit of the Lord put Ezekiel in that bone yard because He wanted him to "mess up" that bone yard. Jesus Himself messed up bone yards. When He died, the veil in the temple was torn in two, a number of graves were opened, and after He arose the saints came out of the graves and were walking around in Jerusalem. Jesus has a way of messing up bone yards!

Many times we look at the situation that we are in, and we find that it is a "bone yard." We must understand that many times the Spirit of God deposits us in those bone yards. I know missionaries that have been deposited in bone yards in Africa, Haiti, China, and all around the world. I know people that have been deposited in bone yards in the United States of America. We have bone yards in our neighborhoods and among our relatives. Even in our families, we find situations that to our natural minds seem unsalvageable. Our mind might tell us to put a black tag on them, leave them alone, and go on and do something that shows promise of life. However, we must always remember that nothing is impossible with God! If we find ourselves in a bone yard I believe it is because God is looking for a resurrection, so He puts someone (us) in that bone yard with a name....the name of Jesus.

The name of Jesus has been given to us, and it is the name that is above every name. When we find ourselves walking among the bones, the Holy Spirit will remind us that we have been given a name to do something about it. Mess up the bone yard!

Prophesy!

What did Ezekiel do about the mess he was in? Ezekiel 37:4 has the answer; "Again he said unto me." What are you saying to us in this generation, Spirit of God? What are you saying to your church? What are you saying to those of us that have been so graciously given a name that is above every other name? That name has been put within us, and He's charged us by His Spirit to use that name. Here's what God told Ezekiel, "....Prophesy."

Many times when we see the word *prophesy,* we think it only pertains to forecasting the future, but this word in the Hebrew language does not exclusively pertain to the future. It actually applies to simple discourse. The word translated as *prophesy* means "to speak forth or speak out." God goes on to say, "....Prophesy upon these bones."

God didn't say prophesy *to* them or *at* them, but rather <u>upon</u> them. The American Standard Version and Revised Standard Version use the word *over.* They say, "prophesy over." The word prophesy doesn't pertain just to the predicting the future, but also to the immediate situation with which we're confronted. This word encompasses every kind of audible expression, including testifying, preaching, teaching, praying, praising and singing. God was basically saying, "Sing over these bones, praise over these bones, pray over these bones, preach, teach, and testify over these bones." He's saying that to people who have been transported by the Spirit into a bone yard of God's choosing and who have been given a name to do something about it, to mess up the bone yard.

Our Bone Yards

God plants churches in certain places to mess up the bone yard in a specific city or area, and he gives us a name with which to do it. It gives us a different perspective when we understand that the situation that we're in which is so ugly, distasteful, and nauseating that we may think, "How did I ever get myself in this mess?" Well, just maybe God transported us there! The Spirit of the Lord puts us in places that without our presence, because of the name He has given us, would be doomed, black tagged for eternity.

We all know unsaved loved ones, neighbors, or co-workers. Dare we embrace the fact that the Spirit of the Lord has put us in that bone yard? I have heard many people say that they could not stand their job because they worked with or for the ugliest, meanest, ungodliest person in the whole company. I myself worked in the business world for a number of years, and one day a man came to me and said, "I've kind of watched your career path and I've noticed that everyone you work for is the meanest person in the company." I believe that I begin to understand that it wasn't due to poor choices on my part, but it was the Spirit of the Lord who placed me under those people. He says to us, "The only thing that stands between that person and a godless eternity is the name I've given you, Now mess up the bone yard!"

If you find yourself in a similar position, pray over the "dry bones." Perhaps that person has reached a point where they don't want to hear you or talk to you, and if you mention the name of Jesus one more time they might explode in anger. Remember, you don't have to speak to them, you can speak over them. You can pray and speak upon them. You can praise God over them and praise God for the fact that they aren't going to die. We just might be pleasantly surprised at how many black tags we can remove!

There is Authority in the Name

God was essentially saying to Ezekiel, "You are in the middle of a hopeless situation. You and your people have been victimized by the godless Babylonians. You think things will never change and there is no way out of your mess. You remember how beautiful the walls of Jerusalem and the walls of the temple were. Your heart is broken, but don't give up because you've been given a name which will invoke the power of the presence of one who can do exceedingly, abundantly above all that you can ever ask or think!"

We must understand the authority in the name. There is power in the blood but there is authority in the name. There is a difference between power and authority. We must have both, but I see in Ezekiel's vision a message, a call, and a challenge to all of us particularly in these last days in this sin-darkened world. We live among many people who seem to be disinterested, distracted, and disconnected from the things of God, but there is authority in the name to change hearts and lives!

There's no book like the Bible, and there is no name like Jesus! We must ask God during the years He has given us on this earth to mess up every bone yard in which He places us. I understand that we are at times conflicted with that question, "Can these bones live? Can that lost person ever be saved? Can that sickness ever be healed? Can that demonic force ever be broken?" Remember the name, and start today prophesying over that bone yard every day; pray, praise, sing, and testify over it.

It's a wonderful privilege to have the hand of the Lord upon our lives, but we must be aware that the Spirit of the Lord may transport us to a bone yard. If we understand and accept that nothing happens by accident and God has divine influence over our lives, we can be confident that we are under the charge of the Holy Spirit to lead us, guide us, direct us, and help us to mess up every bone yard we encounter in the name of Jesus!

The Hem of His Garment

The Gospel according to Mark records an event that occurred near the end of the second year of the earthly ministry of Jesus. He was walking with a man named Jairus, on His way to raise Jairus' twelve-year-old daughter from the dead, when a woman who had been infirmed for twelve years interrupted Him. Mark 5:24-28 declares, "And Jesus went with him; and much people followed him, and thronged him. And a certain woman, which had an issue of blood twelve years, And had suffered many thing of many physicians, and had spent all that she had, and was nothing bettered, but rather grew worse, When she had heard of Jesus, came in the press behind, and touched his garment. For she said, if I may touch but his clothes, I shall be whole." Matthew 9:21 declares, "...If I may but touch his garment" and Luke 8:44 states, "...touched the border of his garment."

Mark 5:29-31 continues the story, "And straightway the fountain of her blood was dried up; and she felt in her body that she was healed of that plague. And Jesus, immediately knowing in himself that virtue had gone out of him, turned him about in the press, and said, who touched my clothes? And his disciples said unto him, Thou seest the multitude thronging thee, and sayest thou, Who touched me? And he looked round about to see her that had done this thing. But the woman fearing and trembling, knowing what was done in her, came and fell down before him, and told him all the truth. And he said unto her, Daughter, thy faith hath made thee whole; go in peace, and be whole of thy plague."

The woman wanted desperately to be free of her illness. She had faith that if she could touch the hem of Jesus' garment, she would be whole. She came, she touched, and she was made whole. Jesus said, "Go in peace and be whole of thy plague." It is important to understand what the Holy Spirit would have us hear and understand regarding this miracle. The word "whole" is translated from the Greek word *sozo* which means "the entire provision of God for the entire person." The Apostle Paul described this in I Thessalonians 5:23, which states, "And the very God of peace sanctify you wholly; and I pray God your whole spirit and soul and body be preserved blameless unto the coming of our Lord Jesus Christ." It is God's desire that each of us experience and walk in the wholeness that He provided. He is everything we need; spirit, soul, and body. This woman decided that nothing short of wholeness was going to satisfy her, and as she pursued wholeness, her body was healed along the way.

Mark 5:25 states that she had an issue of blood for twelve years. However, I believe that her condition was more serious than hemorrhaging, because Leviticus 17:11 declares, "For the life of the flesh is in the blood." Therefore, she wasn't only losing blood; she was losing life. She was literally losing her grip on life, and that is a very frightening situation in which to find oneself.

In his latter years, my father was afflicted with Alzheimer's disease. There were moments when I would look at his eyes as he would search for a word or a thought, but he could not quite grasp it. The thought had been there, but he couldn't bring it back. I saw the panic and the fear he felt because he knew he was losing his grip. For his entire life, he could recall easily and reason clearly, but he was now slipping. It is possible for us to lose our grip on our health, spiritual life, marriage, job, or other aspects of life.

The woman was desperate because she was losing her grip, but she knew that if she could somehow get a grip on Jesus' hem, somehow get a grip on Him, she would be whole. She had done everything she could do to change her situation, but she had reached a point when human ability, wisdom, and strength were insufficient.

Four Steps to Wholeness: Hear, Say, Come, and Touch

The woman desperately needed to get a grip on God, and she did four things, took four steps, as part of the process of pursuing wholeness. The first step is found in Mark 5:27, which states, "When she had heard of Jesus..." Someone, somewhere, sometime told her about Jesus. We should never minimize the importance of speaking the name of Jesus in people's hearing wherever we can. There is power in the name of Jesus, and when people hear it, there will come a time when they will remember that name. The woman's path to wholeness began when she _heard_ the name of Jesus.

The second step she took is found in Mark 5:28, which states, "For she said...." It wasn't enough to hear; she also had to _say_ it to herself. It's Biblical to speak to ourselves. The Psalmist talked to himself when he effectively said to his soul, "What's the matter with you? You're not saying the right things. You're not thinking the right things. Soul, straighten up." (Psalm 42:5). Ephesians 5:19 also encourages us to speak to ourselves when it declares, "...speaking to yourselves in psalms and hymns and spiritual songs."

The third step toward wholeness was that she _came_ to Jesus. Mark 5:27 states she "...came in the press." The Greek word translated as "press" is _ochlos_ and it refers to "a throng of people without order." In life, there are many things to "press through" such as opposition, resistance, and obstacles which can be placed in our way by the enemy. In addition, the press consists of multitudes of well-intentioned, but confused, people. Sometimes we simply have to swim upstream to come to Jesus.

The fourth step the woman took was that she _touched_ Jesus. Mark 5:28 declares that she said, "If I may touch." The Greek word translated "touched" is _hapto_, which means "to grab hold of; to hang onto; to cling to and not let go." She effectively said, "If I can get hold of Jesus, if I can get a grip on Him, I'm not going to let go until I experience wholeness." She abandoned the earthly things to which she had been clinging and got hold of the one person who could give her wholeness and eternal life.

The Prayer Shawl

When studying the Bible, it is important to look at the original languages, Hebrew and Greek, to learn what certain words mean, because modern English words don't always fully describe the original meaning, and the result can be that we misunderstand the Word. In

Greek, the woman would say, "If I but touch the *kraspedon* (fringe or tassel) of His *himation* (garment)." In the Hebrew language, the woman touched the *tsiytsith* (fringe or tassel) of His *talliet* (prayer shawl). There were five items of clothing worn by Jewish males at the time of Christ. They wore a loincloth as an undergarment, a loosely fitting tunic that went from the neck to the ankles, a coat, a sash (both optional), and a prayer shawl. At His bar mitzvah, a young Jewish boy was given a *talliet*, which was considered to be the most important part of his clothing.

The *talliet* was a rectangular garment described by God in Numbers Chapter 15 and Deuteronomy Chapter 22 with certain specifications. A distinct feature of the *talliet* was that it had fringes or tassels at the four corners. The woman in the story effectively said to herself "If I grab hold of the *tsiytsith* and hang on, I will be made whole." The prayer shawl was very important in the Jewish faith. Men wore it over their heads or over their shoulders as a ministry garment to remind them of the importance of the 613 precepts of the Torah. The Torah was the law of God, which we know as the books of Genesis, Exodus, Leviticus, Numbers, and Deuteronomy.

Each letter in the Hebrew language was attributed a specific numerical value. The word *tsiytsith* in Hebrew had three letters, and the numerical value of them was 600. Each *tsiytsith* on the four corners of the talliet had 8 strands and was tied with 5 knots. Adding these numbers together results in 613, which is the number of precepts in the Torah. The negative precepts totaled 365, and the positive precepts totaled 248, for an overall total of 613. Therefore, the *talliet* was a constant reminder to the Jewish people of the importance of walking in and obeying the Word of God. The talliet was actually a symbol of the Word itself. Therefore, when the woman got a grip on the *tsiytsith*, she literally got a grip on the Word!

Power!

When the woman took hold of the *tsiytsith*, Mark 5:30 states that Jesus perceived that "virtue had gone out of him." Please note that the power didn't flow out of the prayer shawl. It flowed out of Jesus. He was the source of the power. The Greek word *dunamis* is the word here that is translated "power" and it refers to the mighty, miracle working power of God. Think of the word "dynamite." The flow of power from Jesus to the woman is significant. Acts 1:8 states, "But ye shall receive power" and the Greek word *dunamis* is also translated "power" in that verse. When *dunamis* power flowed from Jesus to the woman, it symbolically shows us that the Lord imparted His power into His spiritual body – His people. We must begin to awaken to the power that He has imparted to us as His church so that we can stand against the forces of darkness. He commissioned and sent the apostles out to do mighty works because they had the *dunamis* power that was given by Him.

His Power Flows by His Grace

Please note that each *tsiytsith* was tied with five knots. In the Bible, five represents the number of grace. God's *dunamis* power flowed from Jesus through the five knots of the *tsiytsith* and into the woman. This shows us that God's *dunamis* power flows to us by His grace. Ephesians 2:8-9 states, "For by grace are ye saved through faith; and that not of yourselves; it is the gift of God; Not of works, lest any man should boast." God makes it clear that all that we have is by His grace. We cannot buy it or earn it, and we do not deserve it. We receive everything, including power and healing, by His grace. Amazing grace, how sweet the sound!

The number eight in Scripture is an important number which signifies super abundance. There were eight strands in the *tsiytsith*. There were eight recorded miracles in the ministry of Elijah and sixteen in the ministry of Elisha because he had a double portion ministry. When Jesus ministered on earth, He went to the mountain eight times, seven before Calvary and one after. There are eight miracles recorded in the Gospel of John. My book "The Eight Principles of Abundant Living" explains each of these eight miracles. There are eight resurrections mentioned in the Bible, three in the Old Testament and five in the New Testament (three by Jesus' miracles, and two in the book of Acts). The numeric value summed up in the name "Jesus" is 888. The power is in Jesus!

The afflicted woman was very bold and had great faith in the power of Jesus. Under Jewish law, she was ceremonially unclean because of the flow of blood. She had no right to touch anything that was holy. There was a rule among the Jews regarding the wearing of the *talliet* (prayer shawl). A person could only touch it if they themselves, or someone in their family, was the one wearing it. It is interesting that Jesus called the woman "daughter" because it is the only recorded instance in the Bible of Jesus referring to someone by that term. Jesus was effectively saying, "Daughter, it is okay for you to touch Me and receive power because you're part of the family." The super abundant power of God is available to us who are in His family by His grace.

I believe there is going to be a fresh release of the power of God into the church in these end times. I believe this because at Jesus' ascension (Acts 1:8), He effectively said, "I am not going to take the power with me. I'm putting it in my spiritual body (the church), and you will receive dunamis when the Holy Ghost is come upon you, and you shall be witnesses unto me."

When we focus our lives on God, He will make the stories and miracles of the Bible come alive for us. He did that for me as I studied this account of the woman touching the hem of Jesus' garment. I had read and preached about this healing on numerous occasions, but this time I saw something that I had never seen before. I saw that virtue (*dunamis* power) flowed out of Him and into the Body of Christ. We, the church, are the Body of Christ on the earth today. We must accept, embrace, house, and retain His power in order to release it in this age. We must grab hold of the power of God through the grace of God and never let go. We must get a grip on God and His power. There is still power flowing. There is still life flowing. It's available to us so that we can minister with power to others. We must press into Jesus, get a grip on Him, and never let go. The power of God will flow into us and through us by His grace as we get a grip on Jesus and His Word!

Housecleaning Time

During the earthly ministry of Jesus, He performed many miracles, and John 21:25 states that if all of the things He did were recorded, the world couldn't hold the books. We understand that John's expression is called a literary hyperbole which means "exaggeration for the purpose of emphasis." Essentially, John was saying there are many things that Jesus said and did which aren't recorded. Why then did the Holy Spirit choose to record the miracles that we find in the Bible? I believe it is because these miracles contain principles that are vital to our lives today.

As we examine one such miracle, the raising of Jairus' daughter, let us not only rejoice in the all powerful nature of God and the fact that He can do anything, but let us ask the Holy Spirit to teach us truths that will revolutionize our lives.

Signs

In the Gospel of John, the Greek word *semeion* is used to refer to the miracles of Jesus, and it literally means "a sign." When we read of Jesus' miracles, we must understand that each miracle is a sign, pointing to something greater than itself. I believe every one of the recorded miracles literally happened during Jesus' earthly ministry, but they were recorded to deliver truths and principles to us today. The miracles are signs pointing to truths or principles. When someone is driving down the street and sees a sign that warns of a curve ahead, he knows that the sign is not the curve. However, the sign indicates that if he follows the road and heeds the sign, he can negotiate the curve safely. If he chooses to ignore the sign, he could put himself in danger. A sign is very important but is not the thing itself, so when we study Jesus' miracles, we must understand the miracles are very important,

Favorites – Best Loved Sermons from 60+ Years of Ministry

but the principles that the miracles teach us are even more important.

The Bible records three resurrections which Jesus performed during His earthly ministry. He raised the widow of Nain's son (Luke 7:11-17), Lazarus (John 11:1-53), and Jairus' daughter. We will examine the raising of Jairus' daughter, understanding that this miracle is a sign (a *semeion*) which points us to greater truths.

Jairus

Mark 5:21 states, "And when Jesus was passed over again by ship unto the other side much people gathered unto him; and he was nigh unto the sea." Jesus had just delivered the demoniac in the land of Gadara, and then He got into a boat with His disciples and went across the Sea of Galilee to the city of Capernaum. The first person who is central to this miracle story is described in verse 22, which declares, "And, behold, there cometh one of the rulers of the synagogue, Jairus by name; and when he saw him, he fell at his feet."

The Bible tells us at least three things about this man. First, he was a worshipper because he fell at the feet of Jesus. That was the ultimate sign of worship. In that day when a man wanted to worship another, he fell prostrate on his face before that person. Jairus was clearly a worshipper.

The second thing the Bible says about Jairus is that he was one of the rulers of the synagogue, which was a position of special authority in that day. We could consider Jairus as being very much like a pastor of a local church today. He was responsible for the order of the service in the synagogue. He would often read the Scriptures himself or appoint someone else to do the reading. He was the official who communicated with rulers of other synagogues. Therefore, Jairus was a respected man who was involved in the work of the ministry. Jairus was not only a worshipper, but also a minister.

The third thing we learn about him is his name. One of the laws of hermeneutics is that whenever a number or the proper name of a person or place is found in the Bible, it is always significant. When the Bible records a specific name, we must ask what the name means or represents. The name *Jairus* literally means "one who sheds light and shares light to others." Therefore, please see that Jairus is a worshipper, he is involved in the work of the ministry, and he is one who sheds forth light to others. He is a perfect type of all of us who are born-again believers, because Jesus called us the light of the world (Matthew 5:14), and Jesus also said "Let your light so shine before men, that they may see your good works, and glorify your Father which is in heaven." (Matthew 5:16) Therefore, every believer is effectively a "Jairus," an enlightener. We are a light in the world and we are worshippers, dedicated to the Lord, involved in the work of the ministry.

The Gift

Mark 5:23 states, "And <Jairus> besought him greatly, saying My little daughter lieth at the point of death; I pray thee, come and lay thy hands on her, that she may be healed; and she shall live." Let us consider this second person in our story so that we can understand the picture that I believe the Holy Spirit would paint for us in this miracle account. She was a twelve year old girl (according to Mark 5:42) who was the daughter of a believer. Psalm 127:3 declares "Lo, children are an heritage of the Lord; and the fruit of the womb is his reward." The word *heritage* in the Hebrew means "a deposit or gift" so the Bible teaches that children are a *gift* from the Lord.

Hermeneutically, the first time something is mentioned in Scripture, it establishes the type for every other time it is mentioned. The first time children are mentioned in Scripture is in Genesis 4:1, which describes Cain, who was Eve's firstborn. Eve said, "I have received a man from the Lord." She didn't say, "I received him from Adam." She received him *through* Adam but the child came *from* the Lord. Cain was a deposit, a gift, that came from the Lord. Therefore, when Jairus came to Jesus and fell on his face, he was effectively saying, "Jesus, I need help. I'm in trouble. My gift is dormant and dying. Jesus, if You don't touch my gift, it will die. I'm crying unto You to help me because the gift that You have given me is dying. My gift is dying."

It is interesting fact that Jairus' "gift" was twelve years old, and the number twelve is very significant in Jewish culture. When a child moves from adolescence into adulthood, he or she often attends a ceremony that recognizes this transition when boys are thirteen years of age and when girls are twelve years of age. When a boy turns thirteen he has a Bar Mitzvah, which indicates that he has become a son of the law, is recognized as an adult, and can both pray and read scripture in the synagogue. When a girl reaches the age of twelve, she has a Bat Mitzvah, signifying she has reached a point where she is acknowledged as an adult, and she can pray and read scripture in the synagogue. In other words, she reaches maturity, adulthood. Applying this truth to this miracle, Jairus was effectively saying, "Jesus I have a great problem because my gift is dying at the point at which it should be maturing. It ought to be reaching full maturity, but it is lying dormant and dying. Unless you touch my gift, Jesus, this situation is not going to turn around."

Everyone Has a Gift

When we are born, we receive natural skills, talents, and abilities which come to us genetically through our parents or grandparents, and we are unique people because of that. When we are born-again, God gives us a motivational gift in addition to our natural gifts. Our motivational gift is what we often refer to as the urging of the Holy Spirit, or "the unction that leads us to the function." I believe that all born-again believers have a gift. It doesn't matter if they have ever preached a sermon or led a worship chorus. Everyone has a gift and God wants to bring that gift to maturity such that it will glorify Him and fulfill His purpose.

In a local church, God gives the pastor a vision to accomplish a work that is unique to that particular church. He surrounds the pastor with people to help carry out that vision, and as everyone walks in their gifting, the vision is fulfilled. Sometimes, we sit back and wish our church would grow and God would send more people. However, God won't send more people until we all are ready to love and minister to them.

I pastored for almost fifty years and I understand this principle. When we are ready to embrace and help people, God can then do what He desires to do in sending more people into our care. Every person's gift is important, not only to their own personal fulfillment and fruitfulness, but also to the fulfillment of the vision of the house.

Therefore, when a person's gift becomes dormant or is dying, that person and their local church are both falling short of what God wants to accomplish through them.

Jairus effectively said, "Jesus, if You will lay your hands on her, if You will touch my gift, I know the gift will be revived and will live again." Jesus responded, according to verse 24, which states, "And Jesus went with him and much people followed him, and thronged him." Jesus always responds to our cry when we call on Him.

Jairus' Sincerity

Jesus responded because Jairus was sincere about the fact that he wanted his gift to live and not die. I respect Jairus because he didn't blame others because his gift was dying. He could have said, "Jesus, if You wouldn't be so busy doing other things, You would have taken care of me. I am the ruler of the synagogue and I'm so busy that I can't take care of her the way she should be taken care of..." or he could have come up with any number of excuses. Instead, he simply said, "Lord it's me. I'm laying myself at Your feet and declaring that I need you. I'm not going to blame anyone else. I'm going to take responsibility for my gift."

There is a story about two men who ate lunch together every day. One day, one of them opened his lunch pail, took out his sandwich, unwrapped it, and said, "Oh no, bologna!" but he forced himself to eat it anyway. The next day he did the same thing, unwrapping his sandwich, looking at it, and saying, "Not bologna again!" and ate it. The third day he unwrapped it and said, "I can't believe this. Bologna again!" His friend said to him, "Look, if you don't like bologna, why don't you tell your wife?" The man replied, "Wife? I don't have a wife. I make my own lunch." The moral of the story is simply that most of the bologna we eat is of our own making!

Jairus wasn't dishing out any bologna, he was simply facing the facts. He effectively said to Jesus, "I need your help regardless of all these other things going on around me." Jesus responded immediately by starting toward Jairus' home with him. As they walked, Jesus was interrupted by a woman that had struggled with an issue of blood for twelve years. This woman reached out and touched the hem of His garment and was instantly healed. Jesus said, "Who touched me?" and when she heard that question, she acknowledged that she had touched Jesus, admitting effectively, "I touched you. I needed you."

They Said, He Said

Mark 5:34-35 declares, "And he said unto her, Daughter, thy faith hath made thee whole; go in peace, and be whole of thy plague. While he yet spake, there came from the ruler of the synagogue's house certain which said, Thy daughter is dead; why troublest thou the Master any further?" Please note that Jesus was interrupted, and that there were two voices in this situation. Jesus was speaking peace, faith and wholeness but another voice was speaking trouble and death. The other voice was interrupting what Jesus was saying with negative words. The Bible says that the people from Jairus' house came and were speaking trouble and death while Jesus was speaking faith, life, wholeness, and peace.

Many times in my years of ministry I have asked people, "Where did you hear that?" and the response has been, "They told me." I would ask, " Why did you do that?" and the person would respond, "They said I should do that." I've been trying to figure out who _they_ is because it's important to properly distinguish between _they_ and _He_. We can see this a number of times in Jesus' earthly ministry. A blind man named Bartimaeus was sitting by the roadside as Jesus passed by and Bartimaeus began to call to Jesus and _they_ said to Bartimaeus, "Be quiet, you're disturbing things" but _He_ said, "Bring him to me." Bartimaeus was healed because he listened to what _He_ said rather than what _they_ said.

A woman who was taken in adultery was brought into the temple courts. _They_ said, "We caught her in the very act of adultery so we should stone her" but _He_ said, "Thy sins be forgiven thee, go and sin no more." At the feeding of the five thousand, _they_ said, "Two hundred penny worth is not enough" but _He_ said, "Have the people sit down."

When the disciples were out in a boat on the water and a great storm came up, _they_ said, "Carest thou not that we perish?" but _He_ said, "Peace be still. " As Jesus was hanging on the cross dying for our sins, *they* said, "He saved others, Himself He cannot save" but *He* said, "Father forgive them for they know not what they do." At the grave of Lazarus *they* said, "He's been dead for four days and he surely already stinks" but *He* said, "Roll away the stone." Sometimes we get into difficulty and we run to the phone to find out what *they* will say, but if we call twelve people, we could possibly get twelve different answers, and we could be acting based on what *they* said. I suggest that it is better to run to Him and learn what *He* said because what *He* said is often different than what they said. Verse 36 states, "As soon as Jesus heard the word that was spoken, he saith unto the ruler of the synagogue, Be not afraid, only believe." *They* said trouble, but *He* said believe!

Cleaning Out Jairus' House

Jesus, Jairus, and the others with them arrived at Jairus' house according to Mark 5:38, which states, "And he cometh to the house of the ruler of the synagogue, and seeth the tumult, and them that wept and wailed greatly." There were not only mourners in the house but also minstrels, according to Matthew 9:23-26. In those days when someone died, they were laid in state for three days before they were buried. This was the custom because the Jews believed that for three days after death, the spirit of that person hovered over their body, and they could come back to life again within those three days. By the fourth day, however, decay had begun to set in, and the dead person was buried. That is why it is significant that Jesus raised Lazarus on the fourth day after his death, because the people would have known with certainty that he was gone.

When Jesus arrived at Jairus' house, He encountered the noise of mourners and minstrels. Grieving family members often hired mourners, paying them to wail and mourn. The mourners' job was to walk up and down the house and mourn. Minstrels are people that "toot their own horn."

Jesus encountered this house full of mourners and minstrels, noise and negativity, and He effectively said, "We're not having a resurrection in this environment. Before we resurrect the gift we must clean the house. We must remove all of the mourning, moaning, pride and those that toot their own horn. All of the noise must go, because the gift won't be resurrected until the house is clean." Some of the people there were hired mourners, and some were undoubtedly friends and family members. Jesus was effectively saying, "Jairus, you must make a decision if you want Me in the house and if you want your gift to be resurrected. I don't want your house to be filled with all of this junk. I'm not coming in until you make a decision to allow Me to clean out the house." Jairus had already made the decision. He effectively said, "Jesus, I want my gift resurrected. I want you to come into the house."

Mark 5:37 states that there was a crowd of people following Jesus. The verses that follow declare that He put all of the people outside except for Peter, James, John, and the girl's parents. That is a total of five people that Jesus invited into the house with Him. Jesus was the sixth person and Jairus' daughter was the seventh, and since seven is the number of spiritual completion in the Bible, we can see that God was planning to do a complete and perfect work in the house.

Bringing the Gift Back to Life

With all of the noise now outside, the disciples and the girl's parents heard only the Word of God, because Jesus was the only one speaking. Mark 5:39 states, "And when he was come in, he saith unto them, Why make ye this ado, and weep? The damsel is not dead, but sleepeth. And they laughed him to scorn. But when he had put them all out, he taketh the father and the mother and them that were with him <Peter, James, and John>, and entereth in where the damsel was lying. And he took the damsel by the hand, and said unto her, Talitha cumi; which is, being interpreted, Damsel, I say unto thee, arise." Talitha cumi is an Aramaic word which is translated here as "damsel" which literally means "little lamb." "And straightway the damsel arose, and walked; for she was of the age of twelve years, And they were astonished with a great astonishment. And he charged them straitly that no man should know it."

The gift was alive and was again filling the house with joy and happiness. The gift which had been given was now functioning in the way that Jesus intended when He gave it. Jairus was honest enough to recognize that his gift needed to be touched by Jesus. The gift was dormant and dying when Jairus had left the house, and the gift was dead when he returned, but whether the gift was dormant, dying or dead, Jesus' power was great enough to restore the gift to life.

Sometimes the enemy comes to us and tries to tell us that our best days are behind us. He may remind us of our mistakes and failures and try to convince us that we are never going to be used by God again. The devil is a liar! As long as we are alive, it is God's will to bring our gift forth in new abundance and new measure.

Cleaning Our House

As Jesus comes in response to our prayer, our cry, and our plea, He will look at our house, and if He sees anything that's not right, He will cleanse it just like He did at the temple and at Jairus' house. Jesus put all of the mourners and the minstrels out. We go along in life we can pick up negative things in our life. It is human nature. Jesus comes to bless and make alive, not just to restore what we were or what we had, but to make it better than ever before. It's maturity time. We need only look around the world today to know that the time is short. If we have understanding of Biblical prophecy, we know that we are living in the last days. It's time that our gifts come to maturity. It's time that we embrace what we were created to be and do what we were created to do and dedicate ourselves to cleaning our house so that our gift can come alive!

In the Family But Not in the House

Luke Chapter 15 records three parables of Jesus: the parable of the lost sheep, the parable of the lost coin, and the parable of the prodigal (lost) son. Jesus was speaking to a varied group of people consisting of everyone from tax collectors and sinners to the religious leaders of that day. Luke 15:1-6 states, "Then drew near unto him all the publicans and sinners for to hear him. And the Pharisees and scribes murmured, saying, this man receiveth sinners, and eateth with them. And he spake this parable unto them, saying. What man of you, having an hundred sheep, if he lose one of them, doth not leave the ninety and nine in the wilderness, and go after that which is lost, until he find it? And when he hath found it, he layeth it on his shoulders, rejoicing. And when he cometh home, he calleth together his friends and neighbours, saying unto them, Rejoice with me; for I have found my sheep which was lost."

Note that in this parable, the shepherd put the lost sheep on his shoulders to bring him back to the flock. Isaiah prophesied (recorded in Isaiah 9:6) that the government shall be upon His (Jesus, the Good Shepherd's) shoulders, so we can see that the lost sheep was returned through the government of the shepherd. God blesses us when we submit unto, honor, respect, listen to, and follow the ones God has placed in authority over us. We as lost sheep are brought home under the government of God.

Luke 15:8-10 records the parable of the lost coin. The woman who had lost the coin recognized the value and the importance of it. The coin represents that which is valuable in the house like our giftings, talents, and abilities, all of which God has graciously given to us. The women used the broom not to stir up the dust, but to find the coin. Through that discerning work, that coin was discovered and could be used, where it could be applied.

The Parable of the Prodigal Son

Luke 15:11-32 records one of the most well known of Jesus' teachings, and is often referred to as the parable of the prodigal son. This is the parable we will focus upon, and it is the story of a father and his two sons. The younger son went to his father and asked for his portion of the inheritance, and the father divided his assets between his two sons. The younger son took his portion, left home and ventured out into the world, and wasted his entire inheritance in riotous living. Having reached rock bottom, he found himself broke, lonely, and reduced to eating pig slop. At that point, he came to himself and concluded it was better to be at home as a hired servant to his father than where his life had currently taken him. He rehearsed a speech to give to his father and he went home prepared to say that he was no longer worthy to be called his father's son and that he simply wanted to be one of his hired servants. However, before the son had an opportunity to give his entire speech, his father, who had seen him from afar as the son was returning, ran to him and welcomed him with open arms. The father put his robe upon the son, shoes on his feet, and a ring on his finger. The father then directed that the fatted calf be killed so that his family could celebrate his son's return.

The Blessings in the House

We will pick up the story in Luke 15:25, which describes the elder son's reaction to the celebration. "Now his elder son was in the field; and as he came and drew nigh to the house, he heard music and dancing. And he called one of the servants, and asked what these things meant. And he said unto him, Thy brother is come; and thy father hath killed the fatted calf, because he hath received him safe and sound. And he was angry, and would not go in; therefore came his father out, and intreated him."

Please note that the father begged his elder son to come into the house. What was in the house that the father desired his elder son to partake of, enjoy, receive, and be identified with? First, there was _joy_ in the house. There was music and dancing and undoubtedly laughter. Secondly, there was _food_ in the house because they had killed the fatted calf and were enjoying a feast. Thirdly, and most importantly, the *presence of the father* was in the house.

There was joy, food, and the presence of the father in the house, but the son was not inside. An important truth which we can learn from this parable is *that it is possible to be in the family but not be in the house*. We must realize that when we choose not to enter the house, we do not lose our family membership, but we do lose the blessings of being in the house. We miss out on enjoying all that is available to us as our Father's children. As is shown in this parable, the Father will even go to the extent of leaving the house to implore us to come into the house. This is what Jesus Christ did for us in our redemption. He left the house (His place at the Father's right hand in heaven) to come to earth, call to us, and invite us into the house. This is an ongoing process in our personal lives as the Holy Spirit appeals to us from time to time and shows us that the problem is that we are not in the house.

Sometimes we don't discern that the problem is not with the house, but rather with the fact that people won't come into the house and open their hearts to receive all that is available to them. *The problem is that they are not in the house*. We can search far and wide, looking everywhere in this world for joy and fulfillment, but it is in the presence of the Lord, in His house, where we need to be. Psalm 16:11 declares, "In thy presence is the fullness of joy and at thy right hand are pleasures forevermore." Fulfillment and lasting satisfaction are found in His presence. We can face the future with hope and know that everything is going to be alright because He's in the house. We have a right, an invitation, and a call to be in the house. The joy of the Lord is our strength, according to Nehemiah 8:10. As God's children, we have a right to the joy of the Lord. If we grow weak it is because we are not walking in the joy of the Lord. We must be in the house to truly walk in joy!

There is food in the house, and our spiritual food is the Word of God. Searching the Scriptures is not an obligation or a duty, but a true privilege. I thank God for preparing a table for us even in the presence of our enemies. Psalm 23:5 states, "Surely goodness and mercy shall follow me all the days of my life; and I will dwell in the house of the Lord forever." Sometimes we think that dwelling in the house of the Lord forever refers only to heaven, but I believe that dwelling in the house of the Lord also refers to the way we live in this world and the way that we walk every day. We should not be satisfied to simply be in the family. Being in the family is certainly essential, but we should be in the house as well, enjoying the privileges and benefits of all that the Father has for us. The heart of the Father is pleased when we are in the house!

The Importance of Forgiveness

The elder son wasn't in his father's house because he was angry at both his brother and his father. He was angry with his brother for what he had done, and he was even angrier with his father for forgiving his brother. However, his father understood the importance of repentance and forgiveness, and it is important for us to understand this as well. Forgiveness is critical to our spiritual survival and growth. If we do not forgive, God said He cannot forgive us, and that is a heavy weight to bear upon our shoulders.

The Word of God says there are two things that are required if we want our prayers to be answered. When we come to God, we need to both _believe_ (James 1:16) and _forgive_. (Matthew 18:35). When we don't forgive, it hinders our prayers and may prevent the answer that God wants to give us. We are compelled to walk in forgiveness, to not only forgive as an action but to forgive as a lifestyle. It does not matter if the person that harmed us asks for forgiveness, or if we feel that they don't deserve forgiveness. It has nothing to do with whether they were right or wrong. Without forgiveness, we will not enter the house nor dwell in the house.

For years, I wondered why certain people never seemed to be happy, fulfilled, or joyful. These people often went through many of the motions of the Christian life, but something was missing. I learned that it was unforgiveness that was keeping them out of the house. Unforgiveness can impede our progress and prevent our fulfillment in God.

The father went out and begged his elder son, effectively saying, "Son, you must come and enjoy what I have provided for you.

There is a chair for you. The table has been spread for you. The band is playing. It's time for you to come into the house. I am in the house and I do not want to be in the house without you. I have come out here to plead with you to come in." We serve a God whose love is so indescribable that we can't fully comprehend it with our human mind, but we can receive it with an open heart and walk in it.

How Do We Know If We Have Forgiven?

The elder son's response to the father's invitation is important. I believe that I understand the importance of forgiveness, but I asked the Lord one day if He would show me how I can know that I've really forgiven. I can say with my mouth that I've forgiven and think it is so in my mind, but how do I know that I have forgiven in my heart? Jeremiah 17:9 teaches that the heart is deceitful above all things and desperately wicked, and asks, "Who can know it?" We do not even know our own hearts. During Jesus' earthly ministry, He often asked questions. He asked a lame man that had been lying by the Pool of Bethesda for thirty-eight years, "Will thou be made whole?" God never asks a question because He needs more information in order to know what to do. He is omniscient, which means He knows everything about all things all the time. He knows the end from the beginning. He does not have a lack of information, and therefore His questions are never intended to educate Him further.

Why then does God ask questions? He asks questions to allow us to hear what's in our hearts. It's like standing in front of a mirror in which our own hearts are exposed to ourselves so we can see what we truly look like. Most of us, when we stand in front of a mirror, are a bit disappointed because the mental image we have of ourselves is somewhat different than our reflection. At times a probing question can help us to search out our heart.

The elder son gave six responses to the father's invitation that I believe we can use as a "heart test" in situations where we may doubt or question if we have truly forgiven. We do not want our prayers to be hindered. We want the anointing of the Lord in our lives. We will be forgiven even as we forgive. The six things in the elder son's statements, which we can use to evaluate ourselves to determine if we are walking in unforgiveness, are found in Luke 15:29-30.

Principle #1: Unforgiveness Keeps Score

The first part of Luke 15:29 states, "And he answering said to his father, Lo, these many years do I serve thee..." Peter asked Jesus how many times we should forgive someone who wrongs us. Jesus answered, "Seventy times seven," but He was effectively saying that there is no limit, that we must never keep score.

From time to time, we are all badly hurt and deeply wounded, and it is particularly hurtful when we are hurt by someone we really love or consider to be our friend. We cannot deny the reality of hurt, but we must focus our attention on the Healer of all hurt. We must realize that we don't have to even the score, and in fact, we dare not even keep score. When the father welcomed the prodigal son home, he didn't even wait until the prodigal son arrived. The father saw him far off, which indicates that the father had already been living in forgiveness. I believe he lived in forgiveness since the day the son walked out. I wonder if he would wake up every morning and think "Perhaps this is the day." The day finally came when he saw his son off in the distance walking toward home. The son didn't even have an opportunity to ask for forgiveness, because the father had already forgiven. The father could live in anticipation of the restoration and the celebration because he walked in forgiveness.

Principle #2: Unforgiveness Boasts of Its Own Record

Continuing in verse 29, the elder son said, "...neither transgressed I at any time thy commandment." When we boast of our own record rather than being humble, we are walking in unforgiveness.

We try to justify our unforgiveness because we think to ourselves, "I've never done that and I would never do that!" Unforgiveness boasts of its own record and out of that pride comes an inability to forgive. There is no doubt that the elder son was lying or delusional when we said he never broke any of his father's rules, but the father didn't try to correct him. Perhaps he had indeed been a good son. However, the principle is that unforgiveness will always remember its own accomplishments and the good things it has done.

In a sense, unforgiveness elevates oneself about others. We must see it as a red flag when we begin to boast about our own record.

Principle #3: Unforgiveness Complains It's Not Fair

The elder son continued, as recorded in verse 29, "...and yet thou never gavest me a kid." By human standards, it may indeed seem unfair if the elder son never got an animal to roast for a feast with his friends. However, it may be that this statement reveals that he was so focused on blessings from the father that he wasn't putting proper emphasis on the blessing of the father, that is, being in the presence of the father. Our Lord not only blesses us, but He Himself is the highest blessing we could ever receive.

The elder son was effectively saying, "It's just not fair Dad. I've stayed here all this time while he was out there in riotous living, doing his own thing, wasting his inheritance. You never threw a party for me! The good guy didn't get a party, so why does the bad guy get one?" This perceived lack of fairness was preventing him from going into the house. He never was the guest of honor and it was keeping him out of the house. He felt that he never got the recognition he deserved, and it was keeping him out of the house. However, the issue wasn't whether he had a party or not, the issue was that he wasn't in the house. If he hadn't been hung up on the fact that he didn't have a party, he could have been enjoying the blessings in the house.

We must all accept the fact that life isn't always fair, and we must yield to the wisdom of God and place all things in His hands. We won't understand why we are treated unfairly sometimes, but we must put a higher priority on being in the house rather than demanding that our perceived slights be corrected. Life isn't fair, but God is good, and it is more important to be in His presence than to be treated fairly in this world.

Principle #4: Unforgiveness Alienates

As recorded in verse 30, the elder son said, "But as soon as this thy son was come..." The elder son referred to his brother as "thy son" rather than "my brother." When we are harboring unforgiveness, we alienate ourselves from others and distance ourselves from relationships. People will leave churches and do many things in order to distance themselves from people that they cannot forgive. We must always keep in mind that we are all God's children, and as the Body of Christ, we can't afford to be alienated from one another. Our enemy is not another person. Our enemy is Satan and the powers of darkness.

Principle #5: Unforgiveness Thinks of a Person As They Were, Not As They Are

Continuing in verse 30, the elder son said of his brother, "….which hath devoured thy living with harlots." In this exchange, the elder son was the only one that said anything about harlots. In fact, it is the first time the word "harlot" appears in the entire parable. The father didn't bring up harlots and neither did the younger son. The elder son made it a point to bring up the past sins of his brother to the father. However, when he have a forgiving heart, it allows the Lord to show us the way things are, not the way they were.

Principle #6: Unforgiveness Becomes Angry When Others are Blessed

The elder son said, also found in verse 30, "….thou hast killed for him the fatted calf." He was effectively saying, "You killed for him the calf I fed. I've been here taking care of that calf all along. I'm the one that fattened the calf and my brother's enjoying it." Our Father sends rain on the just and the unjust (Matthew 5:45), and we must accept that truth. Romans 2:4 states that it is the goodness of God that leads to repentance.

There may be times in our lives and ministries when we pour our hearts into someone, and they choose to go elsewhere to apply what we have taught them. We must understand that all of the calves belong to God and not to us. If we have the privilege of taking a young believer, teaching them and helping them to grow in their walk with God and in their ministry gifts, and then they leave to exercise those gifts in another church or another place, we should rejoice that God's work is being done. We must learn that God may send us a "skinny calf" that we will take some time to "fatten up." If that calf goes elsewhere and someone else reaps what we have sown, we should praise God for it. We should consider it a blessing to be a part of the Lord's plan in each and every life we have the privilege to touch. We must learn not only to receive but to give. The elder son was struggling with this in his heart.

Releasing Unforgiveness

Please note that father didn't argue with the elder son about all of these things. The son may have had some valid arguments according to our human way of thinking, but he was missing the more important issue, which was being in the house. Even if we have a valid argument, if that argument is keeping us out of the house, it is of no value. Many times, I have had to go before the Lord in tears and leave something at His feet, because more than anything else, I want to be in the house. I can't afford to be without the presence of God, the Word of God, or the joy of the Lord in my heart.

Though in some ways this parable ends with a note of sadness because of the elder son's reaction, we must focus on the parable's revelation of the heart of our Father. His heart should order our steps, direct our thoughts, and lead us onward to victory in spite of whatever we have experienced or faced in life. There are many people serving the Lord decades after experiencing tremendous hurt or pain because they considered being in the house to be more valuable than holding unforgiveness in their heart. When God tore the veil in the temple in two from the top to the bottom, He opened the door and effectively said, "Come on into the house." There is _no_ reason to stay outside of the house. It is our privilege as born again believers to be in the house, in our Father's presence.

We must decide to release all unforgiveness so that we can enjoy being in the house. In the normal course of life, we will encounter things that hurt so badly that it feels like our heart will break, but we must understand that our Father doesn't want us to live with that pain. We must listen to the heart's cry of the Father to leave the pain outside and come into the house. There is room in His house for each of us. We must not only be in the family, but also in the house!

The Ministry of Scars

John Chapter 20 and Luke Chapter 24 both record an account of Jesus appearing to the disciples in the upper room after the resurrection. Both are accounts of the same event, but I believe that each contributes something that is important to the entirety of the message that the Holy Spirit intends for us to receive. There are important principles in this account which we can apply to our lives and our ministries.

Luke 24:36 declares, "And as they thus spake, Jesus himself stood in the midst of them, and saith unto them, Peace be unto you. But they were terrified and affrighted, and supposed that they had seen a spirit. And he said unto them, Why are ye troubled? And why do thoughts arise in your hearts? Behold my hands and my feet, that it is I myself; handle me, and see; for a spirit hath not flesh and bones, as ye see me have. And when he had thus spoken, he shewed them his hands and his feet."

John 20:19-20 states, "Then the same day at evening, being the first day of the week, when the doors were shut where the disciples were assembled for fear of the Jews, came Jesus and stood in the midst, and saith unto them, Peace be unto you. And when he had so said, he shewed unto them his hands and his side. Then were the disciples glad, when they saw the Lord."

According to John's account, Jesus immediately showed the disciples His hands and side, and they knew it was the Lord. John 20:24 records the account of when Jesus came back a second time, "But Thomas, one of the twelve, called Didymus, was not with them when Jesus came. The other disciples therefore said unto him, We have seen the Lord. But he said unto them, Except I shall see in his hands the print of the nails, and put my finger into the print of the nails, and thrust my hand into his side, I will not believe. And after eight days again his disciples were within, and Thomas with them; then came Jesus, the doors being shut, and stood in the midst, and said, Peace be unto you. Then saith he to Thomas, Reach hither thy finger, and behold my hands; and reach hither thy hand, and thrust it into my side; and be not faithless, but believing."

A Pastor's Story

I have a book in my library entitled *A Few Things I Learned After I Knew it All*. The author is Jerry Cook, who was the pastor of a large Bible-believing church in Oregon. Among the biblical truths they taught and practiced was divine healing. During his years as pastor, Jerry had some experiences that were very traumatic. He had a heart attack and underwent open-heart surgery. Then, he struggled with severe depression, which was the result of a chemical imbalance, prolonged emotional upheaval, and the heart surgery. Doctors and the elders of his congregation advised him that he needed a time of rest and sent him away to a retreat in the Rocky Mountains to recover. The Lord faithfully healed and restored him in every way. He testified that he learned many things that he thought he already knew. Reflecting upon his experience, despite the pain and suffering he had endured, he acknowledged that he had a richer life, more balance, with more joy and gratitude than ever before.

After he returned to pastoring, he had an experience that profoundly affected his ministry. One day a man came into his office and told Pastor Jerry that he (the man) was facing one of the most serious things in his life. He said, "I'm scheduled to have bypass surgery and I am very fearful that I won't make it through." Then he said that he remembered having heard about the pastor's experience, and he asked the pastor to do him a favor. He said, "Would you let me touch your scar?" The pastor said, "Certainly," and opened his shirt, and the man ran his fingers over the scar on his chest. He said, "Pastor, they tell me that one of the worst parts of the surgery is removing veins from the legs to transplant. It's painful for many years. Would you also permit me to see the scars on your legs? The pastor consented and rolled up his pant legs. This brother got down on his knees and, once again, ran his fingers over the scars. He paused a few moments, stood up, and with tears running down his cheeks, he said, "Thank you, Pastor, now I have hope. I believe now that I am going to make it. Your scars have given me hope for survival." You see, the scars were evidence that Pastor Jerry had made it through!

Scars Are Evidence of Healing!

All of us have scars in our lives. Life brings challenges and unpleasant experiences, and often times our lives are changed dramatically by these events, and we are never the same again. It may be the death of a loved one, a broken relationship, prolonged physical difficulties, or the loss of a job or a home. We have all done things that we wish we could do over. I confess that I have felt that way about some of my sermons. These experiences leave scars. Sometimes we're embarrassed or ashamed and we think our scars are ugly. However, please note that _scars are not evidence of imperfection; they are evidence of healing_. The scar is evidence that Jesus brought you through the trial!

My Personal Testimony

On my back, I have a small indentation about the size of a nickel where skin has grown to my ribcage. For many years, it was an embarrassment to me, because invariably someone would ask, "What's that?" so I was always concerned about people seeing it.

When the Lord gave me this revelation about scars, it transformed my thoughts, because I saw something I had never seen before and I am therefore no longer embarrassed about this scar. Why? Because of the testimony behind the scar. When I was about two-and-a-half years old, I contracted double pneumonia. It was before the days of penicillin and the doctors informed my parents that there was only one thing they knew to do. They would surgically insert a tube through my back and into my lungs to try to drain the infection. My parents were up, night after night, because I was at the brink of death. Three doctors told them I was not going to survive and they should prepare for my funeral.

My parents were involved with religion at that time, but they were not born-again Christians. In desperation, they searched the newspaper for a source of help and hope, and stumbled upon an advertisement of a small storefront church that said, "We pray for the sick." They took my limp body to that little church. The pastor simply laid hands on me and prayed that God would give me a new pair of lungs. Afterward, they took me back to the doctors who said, "We don't understand what's going on. The discharge of the infection is not flowing anymore. Either the infection has become so thick and heavy that the tube has plugged and death is imminent or, for some reason, the infection has dried up." They decided to remove the tube believing that one of two things would occur; I would either live or die. They pulled out the tube, and you know the rest of the story. Because of that miracle, my parents became born-again, and many decades later, all the members of our family know the Lord and serve Him.

When I look at that scar, I praise God. I am not ashamed of it. It's an opportunity to tell a miracle story and to talk about Jesus. It's an opportunity for someone else to know and hear that Jesus is the Savior and Healer. He is the Restorer, and the Faithful One. I believe it brings encouragement and strength to touch someone who has scars, because scars are a testimony that the person has "made it." When I go through a hard time, I don't go looking for someone who knows all the Christian clichés or will provide easy answers; I look for someone who has scars. I look for someone who has been through something and has made it through.

Jesus' Scars

Have you ever wondered why Jesus had scars after He arose? Why wasn't He perfect in appearance? He came out of the grave with a glorified body that had scars. The Sunday evening after His resurrection, His disciples gathered in the upper room. They were troubled, confused, and fearful, and had locked the door. They couldn't process everything that had happened and they were essentially in hiding. There was a rumor going around that Jesus was alive, but they couldn't confirm it. The only thing they knew was that their vision, their hope, and their entire future seemed to be gone. They must have been thinking, "What do we do now?"

With the disciples behind locked doors, perhaps the devil thought that since he couldn't keep Jesus in the grave, maybe he could keep these men in their own kind of tomb…a tomb of fear and doubt. They could not do much for the Kingdom behind locked doors. Then Jesus walked in, but He didn't come through the door. He didn't have to, because He *is* the door. Jesus showed them His scars. John 20:20 states, "And when he had so said, he shewed unto them his hands and his side. Then were the disciples glad, when they saw the LORD." Undoubtedly, one of the purposes of Jesus showing Himself to His disciples was to confirm His identity. For some reason, Thomas had been absent from this gathering.

However, the next Sunday night, Thomas was there with the others. Jesus knew that Thomas had said he wasn't satisfied with simply seeing; he needed to touch. Thomas had effectively said, "Until I can touch Him, touch His scars, I'm not going to believe." Jesus welcomed that kind of meeting. He effectively said, "Thomas, come here; reach out your finger and put it where they drove the nails. Take your hand Thomas, and press it into My side. I want you to touch My scars."

The Ministry of Scars

If the disciples knew it was the Lord, why did they have to touch Him? This was a group of men who would, in the not too distant future, lay down their lives for Jesus Christ. Ten would die martyrs' deaths. According to historical tradition, some were crucified, some beheaded, and one was skinned alive. One of the sermons Jesus preached is recorded in John 14:19 when He said to His disciples, "Because I live, ye shall live also." As they touched Him, courage and strength flowed into their hearts. They effectively said, "We can face whatever life brings. We can face tomorrow, because we have touched Him, the One who holds tomorrow in His hands." The disciples squared their shoulders, lifted their heads, and walked out of the room that night, never again to gather behind a locked door. The next time they were in the upper room, the Holy Spirit fell on them and empowered them to change the world. God transformed them with a touch.

I believe that touching Jesus' scars was a pivotal moment for the New Testament church. They were liberated from the fear, torment, and confusion that had buried them behind locked doors. After touching Him, they walked out of those doors to meet Satan head-on and to meet the world with a message that Jesus, even though He had scars, was alive. The New Testament church turned a corner that night. During His three-and-a-half years of earthly ministry, Jesus introduced them to the ministries of salvation, healing, and deliverance. He was now introducing them to a new ministry. I call it the Ministry of Scars.

Life brings many things we don't understand, questions without answers, and situations that defy logic. Have you ever been there? We must understand that not everyone can have a pulpit ministry, a prophetic ministry, an apostolic or evangelistic ministry, but we all can have a ministry of scars, because we have touched Him. Others can touch Him through touching us, and we can touch Him through touching one another. Hebrews 4:15 declares, "For we have not an high priest which cannot be touched with the feeling of our infirmities." That means that we have a high priest (Jesus) who *can* be touched with the feelings of our infirmities. He knows about our infirmities, our weaknesses, our struggles, and our difficulties. He understands and He cares deeply about us. He will become involved and heal our wounds.

Touch Him

Some Christians think that those who are involved in fulltime ministry are somehow free of problems. I've been through some terribly difficult times during the years I have been in ministry, but I have learned that touching Him makes all the difference. Every morning I get up, before I do anything, even before I drink a cup of coffee, I touch Him in prayer. When I finish, I have a spring in my step and a song on my lips. I have joy in my heart because I've touched Him. I can square my shoulders and walk out of whatever room the enemy tried to lock me in and say, "Here I come, world. I'm ready for another day."

That night in the upper room, Jesus turned the church around. He released them. He didn't preach a message, but effectively said,

"Touch me and feel my scars, and when you do, be reminded that I rose from the grave, and because I rose, you can make it too." Most of us have been in a place in life where we have cried out, "Oh God, I don't know if I can get through this thing. I don't know if I can make it." God responds by saying, "It's touching time!"

Think about those disciples in the upper room after they had touched Jesus. The world's animosity toward them hadn't changed. The hatred directed toward them from the religious leaders was still as intense. But now, after His touch, they were willing to have nails driven into their hands or their heads cut off, and they would not deny Jesus. They said, "It's okay. We have touched His scars, and we know that because He lives, we are going to live also. No matter what we face, we are going to make it through." I look back at some of the situations in my life and wonder how I made it, and there is only one answer, and His name is spelled J-E-S-U-S. I couldn't live without touching Him, because in the touching, there is healing.

This healing is not limited to physical healing. It also includes healing for emotional, economic, marital, and family problems. We cannot overcome these problems without touching Him. Most people are scarred, but it should not be considered an embarrassment because it's not evidence of imperfection, but rather of healing. We may say, "I had this major problem in my life, and I'm so ashamed. It's so ugly." However, God can use our scars to encourage another person in their desperate situation. We must not let the enemy put us down, destroy us, bury us, and make us believe that our scars are ugly. Through a small hole in my back, I experienced the saving power of the Lord Jesus Christ, which brought my whole family to Him. The scar is not ugly to me anymore. It is an evidence of the grace and healing touch of God.

His Touch

The secret that brings us out from behind locked doors, where we are bound by fear, confusion, turmoil, and misunderstanding, is His touch. The Bible shows us that nothing else turned those eleven disciples around the way Jesus' touch did. Although Jesus is not here in physical body today, He has sent the Comforter, the Holy Spirit, to walk alongside us and help us to touch Him and be touched by Him. Jesus is so wonderful. He touched me and turned my life around, and I touch Him daily to keep me going.

The message I want to share is one of encouragement. Don't look back at those situations, those scars, and think they are ugly. When you think of them, lift your hands and praise God and say "Thank you for taking me through!" Our scars are a testimony to the faithfulness of God. I am thankful for the wonderful, powerful ministry of scars!

The Recipient of Your Gift

In this chapter, we will examine a worship experience that Jesus said would be spoken of throughout the whole world wherever the gospel is preached. It is recorded in three of the gospels (Matthew, Mark, and John) but we will focus on the account which is found in John's gospel.

John 12:1-11 declares, "Then Jesus six days before the Passover came to Bethany, where Lazarus was which had been dead, whom he raised from the dead. There they made him a supper, and Martha served; but Lazarus was one of them that sat at the table with him. Then took Mary a pound of ointment of spikenard, very costly, and anointed the feet of Jesus, and wiped his feet with her hair; and the house was filled with the odour of the ointment. Then saith one of his disciples, Judas Iscariot, Simon's son, which should betray him, Why was not this ointment sold for three hundred pence, and given to the poor? This he said, not that he cared for the poor; but because he was a thief, and had the bag, and bare what was put therein. Then said Jesus, Let her alone; against the day of my burying hath she kept this. For the poor always ye have with you; but me ye have not always. Much people of the Jews therefore knew that he was there; and they came not for Jesus' sake only, but that they might see Lazarus also, whom he had raised from the dead. But the chief priests consulted that they might put Lazarus also to death. Because that by reason of him many of the Jews went away, and believed on Jesus." I pray that will be my legacy...that many people believed on Jesus. That's a powerful testimony to a powerful God. Jesus considered this particular event of such significance that He said "Wheresoever the gospel is preached in the whole world" this story would be told.

The Gathering

This event took place not long before Jesus' crucifixion in the house of a man named Simon in the village of Bethany. Bethany was about two miles southeast of Jerusalem on the eastern slope of the Mount of Olives. Many theologians believe that Simon, who at one time was a leper, had been healed through the power of God during the earthly ministry of our Lord Jesus Christ. The Word of God says that they planned a great supper and invited many important people including Jesus, His disciples, and Lazarus, whom Jesus had raised from the dead.

If we were to enter the room that night, the first thing that would catch our attention would be the aroma of Middle-Eastern foods. The people had gathered for supper and Martha was preparing to serve. As the people mingled and conversed, the resurrection of Lazarus was undoubtedly the center of conversation, as it would likely be if we were to attend such a gathering today.

I can imagine some of the questions that may have been raised. "Lazarus, can you tell us about this experience? What was it like when you died? Did you feel like you were going through a tunnel? Did you see a bright light? Did you see anyone you recognized? How did it feel when suddenly you were back in your body still wrapped in grave clothes?"

The Precious Ointment and the Unseen Worshipper

While informal conversation was transpiring and food was being prepared for the supper, a woman by the name of Mary slipped into the room unceremoniously, uninvited, and unnoticed. Scripture says she was carrying an alabaster box. The term "alabaster box" comes from the Greek word *alabastron* which identifies a container that carried very precious ointment. The container had a conical shape and the ointment it contained was so precious that its value was worth a year's wages. The container's lid was sealed with wax and wrapped with twine to keep the fragrance from escaping. The ointment was made from a root plant called *nard* which grew in the Himalayan Mountains in a far off place that we now know as India. It was very precious ointment, processed and shipped hundreds of miles to the vicinity of Jerusalem. Even today, nard is found in only four countries in the world – India, China, Turkey, and Greece. The root of the plant has a very delightful aroma.

As Mary slipped into the room unnoticed, she walked over to where Jesus was sitting. She apparently had no difficulty getting near Jesus, perhaps because most people were gathered around Lazarus and Simon listening to their testimonies. When she got to Jesus, she broke the container (literally translated, she broke the seal of the container), and began to pour the very precious nard upon Jesus' head and beard. The ointment flowed down over His garments, saturating them, and its fragrance permeated the room. Then, in a very striking act, she dropped to her knees and began pouring the remaining nard on His feet. She then let her hair down and wiped His feet with it, cleaning off the dirt and grime that would often cling to the feet of people as they walked in sandals on the dusty roads in that day. As she knelt there in this deep act of love, humility, and worship, she emptied her nard on Jesus. The Word of God says, "_And the house was filled with the odour of the ointment._" I call that true worship. I call that worshipping "in spirit and in truth." (John 4:24)

Of all our senses, the sense of smell is perhaps the most sensitive to our surroundings. As she poured the ointment, it wasn't long before others that were in attendance began to smell the odor. It is a very pervasive and penetrating odor, capable even of overpowering the odor of the aromatic Middle-Eastern foods that were being prepared for the supper. The people traced the smell to where Jesus was. As they drew near to Him, they were astonished at the sight of Mary pouring precious ointment on His feet and wiping His feet with her hair. Some of them were offended and scandalized, and they began to complain to one another. "What is she doing interrupting this supper and all the plans that we have made?" Some of them became very angry. Judas Iscariot spoke out and effectively said, "This is terrible. This is an absolute waste. That ointment could have been sold for three hundred pence and given to the poor." In spite of all the scandal and unhappiness on the part of the guests, Mary was unfazed. She continued her act of love and worship despite all of the naysayers.

Worship Him for Who He Is

After a short time, as their anger, criticism, and cynicism continued, Jesus spoke out and said, "Let her alone; against the day of my burying hath she kept this." Please note that after Jesus died and His body was taken down from the cross, Joseph of Arimathea brought a hundred pounds of nard to pour on His body to prepare the body for burial. Yet, there isn't one word of praise in the Bible concerning Joseph's gift of one hundred pounds of nard given after Jesus' death. Rather, the Bible commends the woman who brought only one pound of nard, but did so <u>before</u> His death and burial. She was pouring out the ointment in a beautiful expression of heartfelt worship. The people had gathered to talk to Simon and Lazarus. *They had gathered to talk about what Jesus <u>had</u> <u>done</u> but she came to worship who <u>He</u> <u>is</u>.* She poured and poured and poured. I believe that the Lord is showing us through this story that it is important that we give honor to whom honor is due while they are still able to receive it.

There was another person at the table that night that was very much like Mary. His name was John, and he was a unique disciple. His gospel causes us to understand that He was always interested in who Jesus was. Matthew and Luke began their gospels with human genealogies and things related to Jesus' birth. John, however, went all the way to the beginning because he began his gospel (John 1:1-5) as follows, "In the beginning was the Word, and the Word was with God, and the Word was God. The same was in the beginning with God. All things were made by him; and without him was not any thing made that was made. In him was life; and the life was the light of men. And the light shineth in darkness; and the darkness comprehended it not."

In John 1:14, John writes, "And the Word was made flesh, and dwelt among us, (and we beheld his glory)..." The word translated "glory" is the Greek word *doxa*, which refers to His character and nature, and that's what captivated John. John witnessed the many miracles and wonderful works of Jesus. Jesus walked on water, raised the dead, turned water into wine, and multiplied the bread and fish. John was undoubtedly grateful for everything Jesus did, but while everyone else was "oohing and ahhing" over the miracles, John was listening every time that Jesus would talk about who He was. Every once in a while Jesus would make the statement "I Am." In my mind's eye, to modernize it, I see John with his notebook, and whenever Jesus made the statement "I Am," John wrote it down. As he did so, there was a progressive revelation of Jesus Christ, and he was understanding more and more about who He was. I can imagine John saying, "Oh yes, it is wonderful what He's doing, but I'm captivated more by who He is." Jesus revealed Himself many times by using the words "I am."

- "I am the Messiah." (John 4:26)
- "I am the bread of life." (John 6:35)
- "I am from above." (John 8:23)
- "I am the eternal one." (John 8:58)
- "I am the light of the world." (John 9:5)
- "I am the door of the sheepfold." (John 10:7)
- "I am the good shepherd." (John 10:14)
- "I am the Son of God." (John 10:36)
- "I am the resurrection, and the life." (John 11:25)
- "I am the Lord and the Master." (John 13:13)
- "I am the way, the truth, and the life." (John 14:6)
- "I am the true vine, and my Father is the husbandman." (John 15:1)

He carries it into the book of Revelation.

- "I am Alpha and Omega, the beginning and the ending." (Revelation 1:8)
- "I am the first and the last." (Revelation 1:17)
- "And he hath on his vesture and on his thigh a name written, King of Kings, and Lord of Lords." (Revelation 19:16)

It's who Jesus is that matters above all else. What He does comes out of who He is. We thank Him for what He's done, but we praise Him for who He is. We worship Him as we pour our lives, our love, our "nard," on Him.

Dr. S.D. Gordon tells the true story of an elderly Christian lady who loved the Word of God. During her lifetime she memorized many of the scriptures to the point that she could quote much of the Bible. As she began to age, her memory began to slip. She held onto the one verse that she loved most of all, and she would say it over and over every day. It was II Timothy 1:12, the latter part of which declares, "I know whom I have believed and I am persuaded that He is able to keep that which I've committed unto Him against that day." Many people only know what they believe. It's certainly important to know _what,_ but it's even more important to know _whom_.

As she continued to age, more and more of that verse faded from her memory, but she still remembered one phrase which she would repeat over and over again. "That which I have committed unto him." When the time of her passing drew near, her family gathered around her bed. She had already lost her voice, but they saw her lips moving. Thinking that she may be asking for something, one of them put his ear next to her lips and he heard her say "Him, Him, Him." As she aged, she had lost every word of the Bible but one, but in that one word she actually had the entire Bible – "Him." It's all about Him.

Don't Give Your Gift to the Thief

When Mary poured the nard on Jesus, Judas effectively said, "What a waste! This precious ointment could have been sold for three hundred pence and given to the poor." However, John knew the true reason for Judas' statement and wrote about it in John 12:6, which states, "This he <Judas> said not because he cared for the poor; but because he was a thief, and had the bag, and bare what was put therein." Judas was stealing from the money bag. He was a thief.

Please note that _Mary didn't give her gift to the thief_. She walked right by the thief and found the one that deserved her gift. Every one of us has gifts, talents, skills, abilities, and anointing, and we have received everything from God. He gave us some of these gifts through genetics, and others were divinely imparted when we surrendered and committed our lives to Him. The composite of these gift and abilities make up who we are. They are effectively our "jar of nard." Each of us, like Mary, has the choice and the opportunity to empty our jar of nard in love, worship, and service to Jesus.

I have performed many funerals over the years, and I always rejoice in my heart when someone has given their life to Jesus, even if it was in the last moments of their life. However, in those cases, I'm saddened as I realize that it was a life largely wasted because, for the vast majority of their life, the thief was stealing their nard. Jesus said, as recorded in John 10:10, "The thief cometh not, but for to steal, and to kill, and to destroy; I am come that they might have life, and that they might have it more abundantly." Satan is the thief that influenced Judas. Some people tragically pour their whole jar of nard, their whole life, on the thief. Mary didn't do so, as John astutely observed. I believe that is why Jesus said that this event would be spoken of wherever the gospel is preached in the whole world.

We Each Have a Jar of Nard

Sometimes we take that which God has given us, namely our talents, abilities, skills, gifts, and anointing, and we sort of hang them on the wall as a proud display of who we are. Perhaps we even spend our time comparing our gifts with someone else's, thinking, "If only I been given that gift, I would be so much more effective for Jesus." When I was young, I had a passion to sing. I often joke that if I found three guys standing around looking like they didn't have anything to do, I'd form a quartet. Sometimes the groups in which I sang would be invited to minister at churches, and I have to honestly tell you we bombed every time. We were terrible. Finally I got it through my head that I wasn't called or gifted to sing.

When we speak of gifts and talents, we sometimes get the false idea that ministry is only about preaching from a pulpit or singing on a platform. However, ministry is simply living life for Jesus. It's pouring out our nard wherever we are to whomever we encounter. Sometimes we pour our nard with a hug, sometimes with a word of encouragement, and sometimes with an apple pie. When God deposits these things in us, we need to understand that they are not assets, but rather liabilities. They are to be given away and not hoarded for ourselves. We owe it to God and to people to love them and serve them. If I had ten dollars and I deposit it in the bank, the bank is not ten dollars richer. The bank owes me ten dollars whenever I want it. Therefore on their ledger it's written down as a liability. When God graces us with gifts they are His. They are not for us to do with as we please. They are a liability. What a joyous privilege it is to take what the Master gives us and pour it out wherever He sends us.

Luke 12:48 declares that Jesus said, "For unto whomsoever much is given, of him shall be much required." In the parable of the talents (Matthew 25:14-30), the master gave five talents to one man, two talents to another, and one talent to another. He went away, and some time later returned to see what the men had done with their talents. The men that had been given five and two talents respectively both put them to use, and the talents were multiplied such that both men presented more talents to the master than they had been given. The man with the one talent hid it and therefore had nothing more to present to the master than his original talent. That man did not allow the talent to serve its purpose, and the master was not pleased.

We each have been given a beautiful vial of nard that originated not from the Himalayan Mountains, but from Mount Calvary. Jesus is saying to us, "Wherever you go, simply pour it out." When I come to the end of my days, I want my jar to be empty. I want it to be said that I poured it all out. When we pour our nard out on those to whom God sends us, we are pouring it out on Jesus. I believe that was the thing that was so very important about this story. Every one of us has been born with "a jar of nard." We have been given love, time, talents, and resources, and we have one life which we can choose to pour out on Jesus. He should be the recipient of our gift.

Released to Minister

The Bible addresses the topic of ministry in many places, and the account of one particular instance is found in the three synoptic Gospels. This particular event took place during the beginning of the second year of Jesus' ministry in Capernaum, which is located on the northwest corner of the Sea of Galilee, approximately two miles from where the Jordan River empties into the Sea of Galilee.

Matthew 8:14-15 declares, "And when Jesus was come into Peter's house, he saw his wife's mother laid, and sick of a fever. And he touched her hand, and the fever left her; and she arose, and ministered unto them." Mark 1:29-31 provides more detail, and it states, "And forthwith, when they were come out of the synagogue, they entered into the house of Simon and Andrew, with James and John. But Simon's wife's mother lay sick of a fever, and anon they tell him of her. And he came and took her by the hand, and lifted her up; and immediately the fever left her, and she ministered unto them." Luke, a physician, gives us a little more diagnosis of the woman's condition. Luke 4:38-39 declares, "And he (Jesus) arose out of the synagogue, and entered into Simon's house. And Simon's wife's mother was taken with a great fever; and they besought him for her. And he stood over her, and rebuked the fever; and it left her; and immediately she arose and ministered unto them." The word "rebuked" is very important, and it will be discussed later in this chapter.

Three Last Days Truths

I am inspired and challenged in these last days by three significant truths, three convictions I hold. The first truth is that *it is harvest time.* John 4:35 states that Jesus said, "Say not ye, There are yet four months, and then cometh harvest? Behold, I say unto you, Lift up your eyes, and look on the fields; for they are while already to harvest." It's harvest time. If it was harvest time two thousand years ago, can it be anything less today?

The second truth is that in these last days, *God is going to use everyone who makes themselves available to Him*. Joel prophetically spoke of the last days in Joel 2:28, which states, "...I will pour out my spirit upon all flesh; and your sons and your daughters shall prophesy, your old men shall dream dreams, your young men shall see visions; And also upon the servants and upon the handmaids in those days will I pour out my spirit."

The third truth is that there remains a challenge to all of us to *get rid of everything in our lives that would hinder our usefulness to God*. Hebrews 12:1 says, "Wherefore seeing we also are compassed about with so great a cloud of witnesses, let us lay aside every weight, and the sin which doth so easily beset us, and let us run with patience the race that is set before us, Looking unto Jesus the author and finisher of our faith; who for the joy that was set before him endured the cross, despising the shame, and is set down at the right hand of the throne of God."

He effectively said, "Be challenged, that you do not become discouraged or distracted by the enemy, and that you allow nothing in your life that will hinder the full expression of God's purpose, the full manifestation of the reason He has created you." No hindrance — that's the cry of my heart. I believe that the days ahead are going to be the most promising, challenging, and rewarding that we will know in our lives. We must be prepared.

There is something that I see in the record of the healing of Peter's mother-in-law that embraces all three convictions. On the surface, this was a physical healing, like the many healings that Jesus performed during his earthly ministry. The question is "Why did the Holy Spirit select only certain miracles to record for our hearing in the Word of God?" We don't really need a miracle record in order to know that God heals because His Word says He heals, and we believe His Word. I believe that He has recorded specific events to teach us certain principles that are vitally important to the fulfillment of what

He has planned for our lives. I asked the Holy Spirit, "What is it about this particular record that is important for us to hear today, and why did You record it? What is it about?"

A "Nobody"

As we examine this particular healing, we will consider all three of the synoptic Gospel writers' accounts. It was the Sabbath Day, and Peter, Andrew, James, and John, along with Jesus, left the synagogue after the service and went to Peter's home. As they entered, they were told that there was a serious problem in the house. There was a woman, described only as the mother of Peter's wife, that was gravely ill.

This woman was very likely, in the eyes of the world, a "nobody." This is the only reference to her in the Bible and she is otherwise unknown to us. She is unnamed, identified only as Peter's mother-in-law. Also, because she was a woman, she didn't have a highly regarded social status by the customs of that day, and therefore she was unlikely to be the focal point of anyone's attention. She was also unheralded, because there is no record of her particular achievements or accomplishments. She was an unknown, unnamed, unlikely, and unheralded "nobody!" However, when Jesus was made aware of her condition, He gave her His full attention. Every "nobody" is a "somebody" to Jesus! I am so grateful that we serve a God that cares about everyone, regardless of their gender, background, appearance, talents, or social standing. The devil will tell us that we are not important because we have no outstanding talents or we haven't accomplished anything of note. He will tell us we are "nobodies," but *Jesus is attracted to the "nobodies."* As soon as this woman came to the attention of Jesus, she became the most important person and issue to Him at that moment. Jesus didn't say, "We'll get to her later." No, in fact, she became the center of His focus and ministry at that moment.

The Woman's Value

Many people today are victims of the lies of the enemy. They have concluded that they are worthless because of their backgrounds, failures, inabilities, or inadequacies, but they all have value to God! Consider a common a dollar bill. It is essentially a piece of paper, yet it has a value. There is value to this paper. At the grocer or gas station, it is worth one dollar. Wherever it is presented, it is worth one dollar. The value can't be separated from the paper. As believers, according to the Word of God, every person was created by God and born for a purpose. There is value in each life, just as there is value in a piece of paper that is known as a dollar bill. When Jesus looked at the woman, He saw her value. If a dollar bill is crumpled, like some lives, it may not look like it did before, but it is still worth a dollar. If a dollar bill is thrown away, its value isn't diminished; it is simply not being used. Some people have been "thrown away" and rejected by families, friends, and society. They may not look like they did before, but they haven't lost their value. Just like the dollar bill, they've been crumpled, crushed, and rejected, but they are still valuable.

Simply stated, the dollar can be crumpled, crushed, rejected, trampled, and torn, but it is still worth one dollar. Neither a dollar bill nor a person loses their value, regardless of what they've been through, how they've been treated, or how inconsiderately they've been handled. If we settle that truth in our hearts, it will make a difference in our lives, because the devil wants us to look at how "messed up" our lives are, and remind us of all the junk. Jesus saw the value of Peter's mother-in-law as a person, even though she was "crumpled" at the time.

Thus far, we have looked at the woman as a person. Let's now examine her condition. Matthew and Mark both wrote that she was sick of a fever. Luke, the physician, wrote that said she had "a great fever." Please note that Luke didn't say she had a "high fever," and that is because this word "fever" doesn't denote a symptom of a disease; it denotes the disease itself. She didn't have a fever because she was sick; she was sick of "the fever." To understand more, we must understand the types of fevers that were prevalent in that geographical area at the time of Jesus' earthly ministry.

The Great Fever

There were three prevalent kinds of fevers in that area. The first was called the "Malta fever." It was a disease that resulted from a deficiency in the blood. The deficiency could be in the red blood cells, in the hemoglobin, or in the volume of blood. In modern medicine, it would be diagnosed as a type of "anemia." If untreated, the result would be a slow death.

A second kind of fever that was common in that day was called the "intermittent fever" and it was a result of eating or drinking something that was contaminated. We would call it "typhoid fever" in modern medical science.

The third kind of fever, and the most common, was referred to as the "great fever." It was the result of being infected by a contaminated mosquito. It was also called "malarial fever" and we still refer to it as such today. It is a deadly disease unless treated properly. Geography and topography are important to the account of the healing of Peter's mother-in-law. The event took place in Capernaum, which is two miles from where the Jordan River flows into the Sea of Galilee, which is a very marshy area where mosquitoes breed and multiply. In those times, modern sanitation systems did not exist. All of the refuse and the excrement from humans and animals were discarded into what was called a "dung pile." The mosquitoes would feed on dung piles and carry the contamination from it. If a contaminated mosquito bit someone, it could do horrible things to their body. Parasites would incubate in the liver and then get into the bloodstream. Once in the bloodstream and in the red cells, they would multiply, causing the cells to burst. Eventually, the spleen would become enlarged, the kidneys would shut down, and the veins in the brain would become congested. Death was imminent.

I cannot stress enough that this was not a short term malady, but rather a condition which, if left unchecked, would result in certain death. Please note that one of the names of Satan is "Beelzebub" (Luke 11:15), which means "lord of the flies." The word "flies" does not refer to the common housefly. It is a generic term that refers to insects infected by contamination. Satan lives out of the dung pile, the filth of the world, and the filth of hell. Some days, it seems that we can almost hear him buzzing around our heads. The woman in the story was a victim of Beelzebub….until Jesus arrived!

A Rebuke and a Touch

Jesus saw more than simply a sick woman. He saw a woman that had not reached her potential. There was something in her that had not yet manifested. There was a desire, a drive, within her that was suppressed because of being bitten by the infested mosquito. Jesus looked at her, knowing all things, and effectively said, "You can be more than you are." He sees each one of us and knows that there is untapped potential within us.

The first thing Jesus did, according to Luke, was to rebuke the fever. In the Gospels, whenever Jesus rebuked anything, He was speaking to a hostile power. He did not rebuke a *person*; He rebuked a *power*. When the disciples and Jesus were in a boat on the sea and a great storm arose, the disciples thought they were going to perish, because the storm seemed greater than what they or their boat could handle. They finally woke Jesus up, and He rebuked the wind. It was a hostile power. The very fact that He rebuked the fever supports the conclusion that this woman was a victim of an infected mosquito.

Matthew and Mark mention the fact that Jesus touched her hand. Why did He touch her hand rather than her head or her feet? I am convinced that her hand was the instrument through which she was going to fulfill her ministry. Jesus always touches us in the area of our ministry. As soon as He rebuked the hostile power and touched her hand, she immediately arose. She did not simply "get better" from the fever. She was free! It is God's desire for all of us to be free.

Released to Minister

When she was set free, she immediately ministered to everyone present. *Jesus had released her to minister*. Please note that no one told her what to do once she was free. She had a servant's heart, and serving others was something she automatically did. I believe that down deep in her heart there was a desire to minister, but the contaminated mosquito had hindered her. Jesus removed the hindrance so that the desire, the gift, which existed within her could express itself. The Bible doesn't tell us what she specifically did to minister to the others. Sometimes believers have a wrong concept of ministry. They think that one must be on a platform or behind a pulpit to minister. However, we can minister with a smile, a hug, or a prayer. We can minister with encouraging words on the telephone. Ministry does not come from the outside. It comes from the heart. The woman had been born to minister. It was in her "spiritual DNA." When I was pastoring, I loved it when people were ready and anxious to use their talents for the Lord. In my case, until my last breath, I will be trying to bring people to Jesus. Jesus put something deep down in me to minister and I must do all that I can to make sure that nothing hinders that calling. Something more was cured in this women than just a physical ailment. She was released to minister!

Removing the Hindrances

I was born during the Great Depression. My parents possessed little monetarily. In my childhood, I can remember having only a few toys, and one was a teddy bear. I loved that teddy bear. He was a little brown guy with beady eyes and a smile on his face. His little red tongue stuck out, and he was always smiling. They tell me that I used to put my teddy bear in a little rocking chair and preach to him. I may have acquired a slight misunderstanding of what preaching was all about, because no matter what I said, my teddy bear smiled. He never came late. He never left early. What a church! I fell in love with preaching, but later I learned that it doesn't always work with people the way it did with my teddy bear!

I also had a jack-in-the-box. I turned a little crank and watched with great anticipation. Randomly, the crank would release the lid, and out popped Jack! Jack wasn't made to stay in the box, and by turning the crank, the "hindrance" (the lid) was removed. I see this same principle in the woman's story. I see Peter's mother-in-law in the box with the lid closed when Jesus walked in. He rebuked the hindrance and took her by the hand, and immediately she arose and said, "I was born to minister. I haven't been created to be suppressed and confined. I was not made to live in a box."

The infected mosquito, Satan, is still at work today, buzzing around our heads. We've all been hurt, but how should we deal with the hurt? We get healed by allowing Jesus to open the lid. I have heard people say they used to love working for the Lord, but something happened to them which wasn't fair or just, so they no longer serve in any ministry capacity. Who said life was going to be "just" or "fair?" No one involved in the work of the Lord does so because it's easy. It is not easy, and in fact it can be very challenging. We all have to contend with infected mosquitoes, but Jesus can set us free if we allow Him to turn the crank.

I believe that the reason the Holy Spirit recorded this miracle was because He knew we were going to live in a world filled with infected mosquitoes. We must remember that Jesus came to release us, to rebuke every hindrance, and to touch us. We don't know exactly how the woman ministered after Jesus released her. She may have simply made lunch or shared her testimony. Whatever she did, it touched all of them, including Jesus. Suddenly the minister, Jesus, became the object of ministry because the lid, the hindrance, was removed.

I want to challenge you to realize that there is more in you than you have yet seen. I believe God is going to release anointed groups of people throughout the world who are going to change their communities. You have something that others need. Your gift is not for you, it's for others. Christians may use the phrase "my gift," but is that what God meant when He gave the gift? Your gift is meant to be given away. He gave it to you for the Body of Christ, for everyone. In these last days, we are going to see a move of the Spirit of God empowering believers to minister. I don't look for any big heroes in the end-time. I think there are going to be many "mother-in-laws" anointed to minister. By that, I mean God will use ordinary people who have had the lid, the hindrance, removed. We each should remind ourselves, "I can be more than I am. I can do more than I have done."

I believe that the Holy Spirit recorded this miracle because He wanted us to understand that Jesus wants to turn the crank to set us free, releasing us to minister. John 8:36 says, "If the son therefore shall make you free, ye shall be free indeed". We must not allow anyone to come along and try to push us back down "into the box." If we sincerely want Jesus to remove the hindrances and release us to minister, we must apply Hebrews 12:1-2 to our lives, and it declares,

"Wherefore seeing we also are compassed about with so great a cloud of witnesses, let us lay aside every weight, and the sin which doth so easily beset us, and let us run with patience the race that is set before us, Looking unto Jesus the author and finisher of our faith." We must lay aside the hindrances and look unto Jesus. The result is that we will be used mightily by God, and many others will be blessed as a result of each of us being released to minister!

Restoring the Fallen

It is possible for us to understand the things of God, the acts of God, and even the ways of God, yet not truly understand the _heart_ of God. My prayer has always been, "Lord, show me Your heart. I want to have Your heart." I was blessed to be raised in church, and to be exposed to the Word of God and the power of God as a young boy. I know how to "do church," but I want more. I want to know the heart of God. I want to know what He is saying and feeling. I want to know how He is moving and what He wants me to do. Jesus knows the heart of the Father, and that was the key to the effectiveness of His earthly ministry. He said, "I do what I see the Father do," which implies that He could see the Father, feel the Father, and know the heart of the Father. We need that, because we can otherwise make the serious mistake of simply doing good things or doing our own thing, yet not be completely obedient to Him. Obedience is doing His will. That is my heart's cry and my desire.

The Book of Acts informs us that Paul went on three missionary journeys and then made a final trip to Rome. In those journeys, we can see the heart of God for the church and for the world, both then and in our lives today as well. Paul's third missionary journey encompasses Acts chapter 18 through Acts chapter 21. God did great and glorious things through Paul as his ministry was drawing to a close.

One of Paul's ministry stops was in Troas, which was situated on the sea coast in Asia. Troas was a fairly affluent city in Paul's day, but the people there had not been exposed much to the Word of the Lord. Paul brought the Word to them, and resided there for approximately three years teaching and preaching. Acts 20:7-12 records the account of a miracle that God wrought in Troas which resulted in an explosion of the Christian faith in that area of Asia.

The Story of Eutychus

Acts 20:7-12 states, "And upon the first day of the week when the disciples came together Paul preached unto them, ready to depart on the morrow, and continued his speech until midnight. There were many lights in the upper chamber where they were gathered together. And there sat in a window a certain young man named Eutychus, being fallen into a deep sleep, as Paul was long preaching, he sunk down with sleep and fell down from the third loft and was taken up dead. And Paul went down and fell on him, and embracing him said, "Trouble not yourselves, for his life is in him. And when he therefore was come up again and had broken bread and eaten and talked a long while, even until the break of day. So he departed, and they brought the young man alive and were not a little comforted."

A Fortunate Man in the Light

Let us consider more closely the scene on that Sunday night nearly two thousand years ago. Did the Holy Spirit include this account as an indictment against long preaching or as a warning about falling asleep in church? No, I believe there is a much deeper and more important reason. I believe that two of the principles that God is teaching through this account are the principles of *regression* and *restoration*.

One of the interesting things about this account is that the Bible goes into such detail about the facility in which they were gathered and the progression of the meeting. First, it states that they were in an upper room. Many of the buildings in that day were three story buildings. A shop or place of business was sometimes housed in the first floor, living quarters were on the second floor, and the third floor was a large open area that was used for gatherings.

Acts 20:8 states that there were *many lights* in the upper room. The lights were oil lamps that were mounted on the walls and placed in strategic places throughout the room. In this upper room, there were many of these lamps burning oil, giving off heat and light. Because oil is a type of the Holy Spirit, I believe this indicates that there was a sense of the presence of God in that particular meeting, flooding the room like the light from the oil lamps.

One of the listeners, a man named Eutychus, sat in a window. In those days, most windows were simply openings in the wall. The name "Eutychus" means "the happy one" or "the fortunate one." That is a good description of a Christian. We, as believers, are fortunate to belong to Jesus. We are fortunate to be born again. We are fortunate to be headed for a glorious eternity with God. We are fortunate to be forgiven and free from the bondage of sin. We are very fortunate indeed because we belong to Jesus.

Eutychus was not only fortunate, but also happy. He was a happy believer. He knew the provision of God, the joy of the Lord, the goodness of the Lord, and the blessing of the Lord, because names in that day were representative of the nature or the character of the individual. In Eutychus, I see someone who has been touched by God and blessed of God. He was a part of the church, a member of the Body of Christ. He could have been doing something else that Sunday evening, but he chose to attend the gathering of the believers.

Compromise

However, even in the midst of this wonderful gathering, there was a problem, because even though Eutychus was in attendance at this gathering, he was actually half in and half out. Because he was sitting in the window at midnight, he was exposed to the many lights of the room on the one side, but he was exposed to the darkness of the world on the other side. He was essentially located in a compromised place between the light and the darkness. Furthermore, by sitting in the window, he was exposed on one side to the teaching of the Word of God and on the other side to the noise of the streets. This was a very dangerous situation. Exposed to the Word but also exposed to the street noise, and exposed to the light but also exposed to the darkness. Though Eutychus was apparently a happy and fortunate believer, he had placed himself in a position of compromise.

The Christian life would be easier if, once we were exposed to the light, we were never confronted again with the dark, and once having heard the Word of God, we would be deafened to contrary voices. However, there are many voices, not only from the enemy, but also from our flesh, that vie for our attention. We are constantly exposed to *other* noises, but it is important that we make choices that are consistent with pleasing God. Eutychus failed to do that. He was not only listening to the Word of God, but he was listening to other voices as well. Like Eutychus, if we are not careful, we can make the mistake of listening to other voices, such as the voices of criticism, cynicism, and complaint. If we are listening to the wrong voices, we are compromising our relationship with God. Each of us must make a choice and take a stand, saying, "I am only going to listen to the Word of God. I am going to listen to what God has to say."

Eutychus was sitting in the window between light and darkness, between the Word of God and street noise, trying to maintain his balance. It reminds me of an experience I had when I was standing on a dock and stepped with one leg into a boat that wasn't tied to the dock. The boat was moving one way, and the dock was not moving at all. Welcome to the world of the falling!

The Process: Slumping, Then Falling

Eutychus was sitting there, listening to Paul preach. Granted, Paul was preaching a long time. It was midnight, and he hadn't yet finished. The Bible describes Eutychus' regression. It doesn't say, "All of a sudden, he fell." It also doesn't say that someone pushed him. It says first he *slumped* (sunk) down, and then he *fell* down. I believe it is important to recognize that we don't fall down without first slumping down. There was a *regression* taking place.

Eutychus was regressing from a place of alertness to a place of relaxation and finally to a place of deep sleep. Medical science tells us that we all go through degrees of alertness according to the way our brain is functioning. The brain actually functions in cycles per second. If we are hassled, hurried, frustrated, or very excited, our brain cycles over twenty-one cycles a second. When we are in a more "normal" state, we are alert, receptive, and responsive, and the brain cycles between fourteen and twenty cycles a second. This is called the alpha stage of brain function. If we begin, as Eutychus did, the process of slumping or sinking down, the brain's cycles per second decrease to between six and thirteen. This is considered a relaxed state where we are "_there, but not really there_." The next step of regression is deep sleep, when the brain is only cycling three to five cycles per second. That's where Eutychus found himself. His brain cycles were decreasing and he was in a state of regression. He was there, but he was not there.

The process of descending into sleep is worthy of note. From the state of hearing words and understanding them clearly, we can descend to the state of hearing words but failing to understand the meaning. As the descent continues, we no longer hear distinguishable words, only noises. We know someone is talking but we have no idea, nor even care to know, what they are saying. In the final stage, we no longer even hear noises. This is a normal process in the physical realm of a person's life. This is how we "fall" asleep.

However, this is an unwelcome and devastating process in a person's spiritual life. In chapters 2 and 3 of the Book of Revelation, Jesus cautioned the church seven times about such a possibility. He said, "He that hath ears to hear, let him hear what the Spirit saith to the churches." To hear the Word of God without impact, conviction, or change, is very sad and potentially devastating.

Eutychus had _regressed_ from alertness to sleep during the period of time he was in the meeting. This is a picture of the spiritual condition in our world today. Jesus said, as recorded in Matthew 24:12, "Because iniquity shall abound, the love of many shall wax cold." Another translation says "grow cold" and yet another says "_cool off._" This refers to regression. Because the darkness is so strong, the light can begin to fade out and we can regress. In II Thessalonians 2:3, Paul declares, "Let no man deceive you by any means before that day come." Paul was referring to the coming of the Lord. Before Jesus comes again, he stated, "There shall come a _falling away_ first."

In II Timothy 3:1 Paul declares, "This know, In the last days, perilous times shall come." It's interesting that he didn't speak of nuclear or biological warfare when referring to perilous times. Instead, he spoke of the condition of the hearts of men. Paul stated, "Men shall be lovers of their own selves, trucebreakers, incontinent." Verse 5 declares, "Having a form of godliness, but denying the power thereof."

This doesn't mean denying in the sense of saying "I don't believe it's true." It means denying in the sense of "walking away from something that you once had." Another word for it is *"forsaking."* Staying on fire for God is not easy. We must work at it. Many distractions from the world are undoubtedly going to come against us.

Eutychus, our happy brother, had slumped into total sleep. The only thing remaining after we _slump_ down is to _fall_ down. I want to be so sensitive that if I see people spiritually slumping, I want to go to them, talk to them, and pray for them in the hope that their regression will be halted. I don't want to wait until they fall. I don't want to see them in the state in which Eutychus found himself.

Paul Shows the Heart of God

When Eutychus fell, Paul had reason to react differently than he did. Paul could have become offended. He could have said, "I am tired and weary. I've been teaching and preaching for hours, giving everything I have, and Eutychus falls asleep on me and then literally falls. I guess that serves him right." Paul could also have simply concluded, "We didn't need him anyway. The room is already full. What does one listener matter?"

Be reminded that the heart of Jesus was so touched with the one lost sheep that He left the other ninety nine sheep to search for the one that was lost (Luke 15:4). I see the same heart in Paul. I don't know how many people were in the room listening to Paul teach that night, but he cared about the one man that was struggling. He cared about the one who chose to sit in the window and who eventually fell. I believe that the heart of God was made manifest through Paul. Paul stopped preaching because he cared about each and every person, and he wanted to take care of the need that had arisen. I have to commend the Christians that were there because they didn't all get up and leave when Eutychus fell. Paul had already preached a long time and it was midnight. They could have seen this interruption as a chance to leave, but they didn't. They were patient as Paul suspended the meeting and responded to Eutychus' desperate need.

Eutychus lay outside on the ground with a broken neck. The Apostle Paul, not offended, not forsaking a brother, reminds me of what he wrote in Galatians 6:1. Paul not only wrote this, but he lived it. He wrote, "Brethren, if a man be overtaken in a fault ye which are spiritual restore such a one in the spirit of meekness." This is the Bible definition of what it means to be spiritual. It isn't defined by seniority, by how many songs we can sing, or how many Scriptures we can quote. It is defined by the condition of our heart. God effectively said that if we are spiritual, we will be _restorers_.

"Restore such a one in the spirit of meekness." Paul didn't go down to the man lying there with a broken neck and say, "I told you not to sit in the window. I knew that was going to happen." That is not "in the spirit of meekness." Paul goes on to write, "Considering yourself, lest you also be tempted." He is saying that every one of us have the potential of slumbering, slipping, and falling. We must remember that truth when we are ministering restoration! We must not look _down_ at the person, but rather, look _across_. We mustn't hit him on the head, but instead give him a helping hand. We must not tell everyone what he did wrong, but rather take it to Jesus. We must fall on our face at the foot of the cross and pray about it.

Paul Went Down to Him

Paul continued his thought in Galatians 6:2, which states, "Considering yourself, lest you also be tempted." In Troas at midnight, Paul had a brother, Eutychus, who was overtaken in a fault, who fell asleep and then literally fell because he didn't pay attention. What is the first thing Paul did? He _went down to the fallen one_. This demonstrates the heart of God toward a fallen one. Paul could have acted "super spiritual," leaned out of the window high above Eutychus, and said, "Dear brother, in the name of Jesus, get back up here." However, God is showing us through Paul's actions that there comes a time when we must go down to the fallen one and meet him right where he or she is. We must feel what they feel and hurt as they hurt. Paul went down to where Eutychus was. He was effectively saying, "I am not too great or too important to go down to the fallen one." We aren't told how Paul interrupted or suspended his teaching after Eutychus fell. Paul may have said, "Folks, please bear with me for a moment. I will be right back. I must bring one of our brothers back."

Sometimes the Holy Spirit interrupts a gathering to reach out to one person.

Paul went down to where the fallen man was. I believe deep down in his spirit Paul was saying, "Devil you're not going to take one of us. You're not going to take one of ours. You're not going to take one for whom Jesus died. You're not going to even get one of them, devil."

Paul Fell On Him

Paul went down to Eutychus, and then he _fell on him_. He not only went to where Eutychus was, but he also identified with his condition. After someone has fallen three floors and is lying there with a broken neck, he is undoubtedly an unpleasant sight. Eutychus was likely not only dirty but very bloody, but Paul wasn't afraid to identify himself with this broken man. When Paul fell on him, the life that was in Paul began to be imparted into the man. The death in the man was not coming into Paul, but the life in Paul was going into the dead man. Life is greater than death. Light is greater than darkness. "The light shineth in darkness and the darkness comprehended it not." (John 1:5). Paul fell on him, and in doing so, he was effectively saying, "Eutychus, I care about you. God placed you here with us, and we need you. I identify with you brother. You don't belong down here. You belong up there where we have been enjoying God's presence. You belong up there in the Word of God. You belong up there in prayer and in praise. You weren't created to be down here."

Paul Embraced Him

The third thing Paul did was embrace Eutychus. He went down to him, he fell on him, and he _embraced_ him. The word "embraced" means "to have compassion and to intercede for." There are times when one simply commands "In the name of Jesus, rise and walk," like Peter and John did going into the temple (Acts 3:6), but embracing someone is often more challenging than commanding them. There may be times the Lord instructs us to command, but there are also times when He calls us to embrace and hold the fallen one until the life that is in us flows into them.

Paul put his arms around Eutychus, picked him up, and held

him. The Word of God says that Eutychus had already been pronounced dead. Studying the entire context of this passage reveals that, in all probability, Luke, the writer of the Book of Acts, was on this third missionary journey with Paul. It follows then that, as a physician, Luke had already examined Eutychus and declared he was dead. Furthermore, the Greek word is very clear that Eutychus was dead. However, Paul knew that God is the God of life, so he embraced Eutychus. The Greek word infers resuscitation. Paul held Eutychus and breathed into him!

The Holy Ghost was in Paul so he breathed the breath of life. Prior to Paul's conversion, he went about breathing threats and death against the Christians. Then, he was breathing death, but now he was breathing life. Paul wrote about that in Ephesians 4:29, "No corrupt communication shall proceed out of your mouth but that which is good for the use of edifying." We either breathe life or we breathe death.

Paul took him by the hand and they walked back up into the meeting, and it turned into a revival! The people were full of joy because Eutychus had been rescued and restored, and he was again together with the family to which he belonged. I can only imagine the atmosphere in that upper room when Paul came walking back in, not to have a funeral, but with a spring in his step, joy in his heart, and Eutychus at his side!

The Bible doesn't state that Eutychus went up and sat in the window again. Once we understand that the place of compromise between light and darkness is a dangerous place to be, we will not go back to it. If we compromise between what the Lord says and what the world says, it affects where we choose to sit. Ephesians 2:6 declares that we are called to "sit together in heavenly places in Christ Jesus."

Restoration

The unfolding of this miracle reveals, illuminates, and displays the heart of God to us. Unquestionably, the heart of God is for *restoration*. Restoration is very important, because unless we are restored, we can't be a part of what God is doing. Restoration is necessary because we live in a world in which sin abounds, and there is an ever present danger of falling, perhaps even multiple times. Regardless of how many times we fall, the solution is to be restored back to God.

For a time, Eutychus ceased to be a part of what God was doing in that upper room. Eutychus was physically present but no longer "there," no longer "tuned in," no longer involved. He hadn't committed any great sin. He hadn't purposely decided that he was going to have no part in the things of God or have nothing to do with what God was all about. He was simply in regression and he fell, but God worked through Paul to bring restoration!

Restoring the Fallen

There are a great number of people that once walked with the Lord but have fallen away and need to be restored. I believe wholeheartedly in end time revival. I believe that there will be a restoration of many that have fallen away. I believe children are going to be restored to their parents. I believe that there is going to be a restoration of those that have been hurt and wounded, cast aside, and rejected. The Lord has not forgotten any of them.

Joel prophesied that restoration would be prevalent in the end times. In Joel 2:25, referring to the last days, God declares, "I will restore unto you the years that the locust hath eaten, the cankerworm, the caterpillar, and the palmerworm..." I want to put the emphasis on "restore." God is effectively saying, "One of the things I am going to do in the last days is restore everything that needs restoration." The revival fire of God is going to be so evident in the last days that it will awaken, quicken, and startle. It is going to shake everything that can be shaken. There will be a day of judgment, to be certain, but the heart of God today is to _restore_. I want to be restored and I want to be a restorer, because that's the heart of God. I believe that if every person who ever confessed Jesus as Lord or has been a part of a church, turned back to God, there would not be enough churches to contain all the people!

Our mighty God is on the throne and, through His people, He is in the work of restoration. _I am convinced that the power of restoration is greater than the power of regression._ I believe there is coming a breaking loose of the chains that tie, the bands that hold, and the forces that resist, and there will be a turning back to God.

Jesus Christ will return someday, possibly soon, but I do not believe that we're called to simply wait for His return and do nothing. I believe we are placed here for a purpose and gifted according to His perfect will so that we can stand and resist *regression* in the name of *restoration* and see a mighty turning back to God on the part of the people of God. We are called to restore the fallen!

My heart beats for restoration. I dream about it, I think about it, and I pray about it. I believe it's the heart of God. God is looking for a group of people that will lay aside their own plans and agendas and who will touch people where they are, embrace them, and breathe into them the word of life until they are restored and made whole. This is a day of restoration!

The devil will tell us that someone has sunk too deep, fallen too far, or have been gone too long. The devil is a liar. He was a liar from the beginning and he hasn't changed his ways; he's still a liar. He would like us to think that *regression* is greater, but the blood that flowed from that old rugged cross cried *restoration*!

The devil tries to bring pain and destruction into the lives of people. He brings things that are so hurtful, painful, and indescribable that people can't see tomorrow or feel like there is any reason for living. However, the Word of the Lord is that there is hope! Paul didn't turn his back on Eutychus or consider him hopeless or worthless. He restored Eutychus into the fellowship of believers, and the people were so excited that Paul preached till dawn. What had affected these people? *They learned that restoration was greater than regression.* Likewise, today is a day of going to where the fallen people are, identifying with them, and saying, "I love you. We're going to make it together. You don't belong to Satan. You belong to God."

If you have wayward children that have slipped away, don't give up on them. If you dedicated them to Jesus, they belong to Jesus. Tell the devil to take his hands off God's property. They may have made a mess of their lives, but that's not the end of the story. The end of Eutychus' story is he went back up the stairs and had communion, and experienced perhaps the greatest service they ever held. God is

Favorites – Best Loved Sermons from 60+ Years of Ministry

alive, and there is none like unto Him.

God Can Keep Us from Falling

Even greater news is that it isn't necessary for us to fall. Jude 24 declares, "Unto Him that is able to keep us from falling and to present us faultless before His throne with exceeding great joy." God keeps us from falling by getting our attention when we begin to slump. When we start slumping, He nudges us gently or takes more aggressive action, depending on what is needed to "wake us up" and therefore keep us from falling. We may say, "God, quit picking on me." He says, "I love you too much to let you slump and fall. I will deal with you while you are slumping so that we can prevent the fall. I want you to sit up straight and get serious about our relationship. Shake off everything that is slowing you down." Hebrews 12:1 declares, "Wherefore seeing we also are compassed about with so great a cloud of witnesses, let us lay aside every weight, and the sin which doth so easily beset us, and let us run with patience the race that is set before us." It declares, "Let us lay aside every weight." The weights are the things that make us slump. I decided many years ago that I cannot afford to carry the weight of unforgiveness or criticism in my heart. I need the anointing too badly.

It is time for us to realize that God is in the restoring business. He is awakening and anointing His church because our world is filled with people that have fallen. Some people who once praised God, studied their Bible, and worshipped Him, are walking in darkness today. They have fallen, but God loves them and wants them restored. Lord, let us be an oasis in the desert, a place where the weak, weary, broken, and blind can come and find life and love, and be restored. Lord, help us to embrace and bring back into the fold those who have slumped and fallen. We want to have Your heart to restore the fallen.

Where Art Thou?

It was the last time Jesus would pass through Jericho before He went to Calvary. Jericho was a very prosperous city which was often referred to as a city of sin and gross darkness, yet Jesus didn't exclude Jericho from His plan and His journey. There was a man named Zaccheus in Jericho whose encounter with Jesus reveals to us another dimension and expression of the unfeigned love of God.

Luke 19, starting in verse 1, states, "And Jesus entered and passed through Jericho. And, behold, there was a man named Zaccheus, which was the chief among the publicans, and he was rich. And he sought to see Jesus who He was, and could not for the press, because he was little of stature. And he ran before and climbed up into a sycamore tree to see Him, for He, Jesus, was to pass that way. And when Jesus came to the place, He looked up and saw him and said unto him, Zaccheus, make haste, come down, for today I must abide at thy house. And he made haste and came down and received Him joyfully. And when they saw it" – that is, the people that were standing there with Him, some religious leaders, some disciples – "when they saw it, they all murmured, saying that He was gone to be guest with a man that is a sinner. And Zaccheus stood and said unto the Lord, Behold, Lord, the half of my goods I give to the poor, and if I have taken anything from any man by false accusation, I restore him fourfold. And Jesus said unto him, This day is salvation come to this house, forsomuch as he also is a son of Abraham." Verse 10 declares, "For the Son of Man is come to seek and to save that which was lost."

Despised Occupations

In Israel, during the time of the earthly ministry of Jesus, there were a number of vocations that were identified by the religious leaders as undesirable, and many of the young men were instructed not to pursue these professions because these occupations were so dishonorable and unethical. In fact, the religious leaders grouped the undesirable professions into three categories. One category was called the "despised" occupations. Two of the occupations on the list of the despised were the physician and the butcher. They were called "despised" because these occupations gave special attention to the rich and ignored the poor, so they were felt to be unjust and unfair. There is absolutely nothing inherently wrong with the occupation of physician or butcher. Thank God for good and Godly physicians. Luke himself, the author of the books of Luke and Acts, was a physician. He traveled with Paul. There is nothing wrong with the occupation itself as long as it is practiced justly and honestly, but young men were told not to pursue that profession because there was so much injustice and unfairness.

Dishonorable Occupations

A second category was called the "dishonorable" occupations. Among those particular occupations were the "tanner of dead animal skins," the "dung collector," and the "garbage collector." Young men were told, "Don't get involved in those occupations. They are unclean and dirty." There was even a legal provision which allowed a wife to divorce her husband if he was employed in one of these professions.

Immoral Occupations

A third category, and the one I will address in greater detail, was called the "immoral" occupations. These were not just dishonorable, not just despised, but immoral. There were four professions listed in this category, two of which involved gambling. The first was a person that gambled with dice. A second was a man that trained pigeons which were used for pigeon races, which men gambled on. A third was called the occupation of "usury," in which someone would loan money at high interest rates. It was considered immoral because most of the people that were involved in that practice took advantage of the poor. The fourth occupation that was considered immoral was the "tax collector." If you were a dung collector, a tanner, a gambler, a pigeon trainer, or someone in the profession of usury or tax collector, you were despised. It's interesting that such focus would be on the particular occupation of tax collector. It's also interesting how Jesus dealt with tax collectors during His earthly ministry, and how He did not exclude them from the plan and love of God.

The Tax Collector

The occupation of tax collector came about because much of Israel was occupied by the Romans at that time, and it was the desire of the Roman Empire to squeeze all of the money out of Israel that it could. They did it by any means, regardless of whether it was fair, legal, or just. Their whole system of taxation was corrupt. Rome delineated certain geographical regions, and then put the tax collection position for each region out for bids. The "bid" was the amount of money that the tax collector promised to collect for Rome. Anyone could bid to be the tax collector for a region. Sometimes the bidders were Romans, but frequently they were Jews. The highest bidder had to pay Rome the agreed upon price, but everything that he collected over and above that amount he kept for himself. As you can imagine, all kinds of scheming and evildoing came into practice.

Tax collectors came to be known as people that were out to steal from the people. They were considered thieves, and they would take everything they could from the people. The Jewish people considered them traitors because they sold themselves out morally to Rome and, in the name of greed, cheated their own families and neighbors. Anything was acceptable to them in the name of profit, so these people were absolutely despised. It was commonly said in Israel that "repentance is very hard for a tax collector," and many people believed it was impossible. Certain political and social limitations were placed on tax collectors. For example, tax collectors were forbidden to be witnesses in a court of law because they were considered to be too dishonest. Secondly, they were forbidden to be judges because of the stigma associated with the occupation. Thirdly, very devout Jews would take great care that even the hem of their garments would not touch the hem of the garment of a tax collector. In general, people stayed away from tax collectors, considering them to be evil, corrupt traitors.

Zaccheus

In that context, the Holy Spirit takes the searchlight of heaven and shines it on a man who was not only a tax collector, but a *chief* tax collector. He was so good at his trade that he had responsibility over other tax collectors. He knew all the tricks of the trade, and he was apparently a good schemer. His name was Zaccheus. Obviously, his parents had no idea how he was going to turn out, because they named him Zaccheus, which means "pure and justified." As a tax collector, he was anything but pure and justified. We don't know much about him except for one physical characteristic that the Bible identifies. He was very short; what some might call "vertically challenged." That is all we really know about him, aside from the fact that he was a very successful tax collector. Evidently, as a young man, he had disregarded all of the recommendations of his elders and had gone into this very corrupt occupation. For the love of money, he became unconcerned about having close friends or being accepted by his neighbors or his family.

Jesus, the Son of God, the most pure, just, honest, and holy man that has ever lived, had no problem with tax collectors. In fact, He had already chosen one of them, a man named Matthew, to be part of His group. Jesus walked by the gate of the city one day, looked at Matthew (also called Levi), and said, "Follow Me. Don't lay down your pen. You can leave your books, but hang onto your pen because we are going to use that later. You are going to write a book for Me." Can you imagine what must have gone on among the group of disciples? They were very zealous. They were dedicated Israelites, and to accept Matthew into the group was not easy, because tax collectors were so despised. Jesus said, "I want you," and Matthew left everything to follow Him. Matthew was so excited about being chosen by Jesus that he threw a party for all his tax collector friends, and Jesus went to the party!

Through this, God is showing us a new dimension of His heart and His love. Jesus didn't seem to have any problem with those whom other people despised. Zaccheus heard that Jesus was going to pass through Jericho, and he was curious. I believe that Zaccheus wanted to see the kind of man that would hang out with people like him. "I must see this one called Jesus because I have heard He hangs out with tax collectors. I heard that He goes to parties with tax collectors." Zaccheus was conflicted, because he had a desire to see Jesus, but on the other hand, he had a concern about being seen *by* Jesus. Zaccheus may have thought, "How can I see Jesus without Him seeing me? He is coming this way. I will climb up into a tree, where I can get a good view of Him, but at the same time I will limit how close He gets to me." Zaccheus knew that he was unworthy. He decided to climb up into a sycamore tree.

Hiding in the Sycamore Tree

A sycamore tree is a cross between a mulberry tree and a fig tree. It is the size of a mulberry tree, about eight feet in circumference, but it has the fruit of a fig tree. In that day, people would line the roads with sycamore trees for two reasons. One was to make the area more beautiful, and the other reason was to provide food for the people that were poor. If you couldn't afford to buy food, you could walk along the road and partake freely of the figs on the sycamore trees without cost. Here is Zaccheus, a very rich man, up a poor man's tree. God sure has a sense of humor! I can imagine this little man peering through the fig leaves wanting to see Jesus. "I must get a closer look at this man, but it's hard to hide behind the fig leaves and still see."

Adam tried hiding behind fig leaves after he and Eve had sinned. As soon as they realized they had failed God, they were afraid and became ashamed of their nakedness. In their shame, they covered themselves with fig leaves (Genesis 3:10) which were totally inadequate. It's no wonder the only tree on record that Jesus cursed during His earthly ministry was a fig tree. It represents the hiding place. It is where you hide when you don't want to be seen, when you are ashamed of yourself, when you feel unworthy and inadequate, when you feel like a failure. Adam said, "I was afraid when I saw I was naked, and I hid myself." Like Adam and Eve, Zaccheus also hid behind fig leaves.

This is a picture of human nature, which tends to run to fig leaves instead of running to Calvary. Zaccheus, in his fallenness, in his failure, in his weakness, thought the same thing that Adam thought and that every other person has thought: "If God sees me like I really am, He will not love me."

Is that not the reason we hide? We hide for fear that if the shame of our "nakedness" is apparent, we will not be loved. We say, "If they only knew what I was really like, they wouldn't love me." Have you ever thought that? We hide, but it's a deception of the enemy, because the love of God isn't like the love of men. When God came into the garden looking for Adam, He wasn't looking to condemn him. He was interested in restoring the closeness they once enjoyed.

Time to Come Out of Hiding

How often we hide. We hide behind our language. We know what to say and when to say it. We know what songs to sing and when to clap our hands in church. We hide behind our busyness. We hide behind our friends. We are always hiding. It appeared that Zaccheus was successful in his hiding, except that as Jesus got closer to that tree, He suddenly stopped. Picture a whole group of people following Jesus. When He stopped, they stopped. "Why is He stopping here?" Then they saw Him look up into that tree. "What is He looking at?" "I don't know. It looks like a little kid up there." Jesus says, "Zaccheus!" Talk about being identified! Jesus could have said, "You up there," but instead He called Zaccheus by name. "Zaccheus, get down from there right now." I can imagine some of the very devout people saying, "Oh boy, he is going to 'get it' now! Payback time. That little guy deserves it. He ripped me off. Get him, Jesus." Jesus said, "Do you think you can hide from Me? I have been searching for you." In Genesis 3:9, God said, "Adam, where art thou?" Do you think for a minute that God didn't know where Adam was? He knew exactly where he was. He just wanted Adam to admit where he was.

Jesus was saying to Zaccheus, "The day of hiding is over. The day of shame is over. The day of walking around with your head down is over. I am coming by your tree today. You have been up in the tree too long." The next thing He said is one of the most powerful things that could ever be said. He said, "Zaccheus, I want to go abide at your house." I believe there are two reasons He said that. First of all, Jesus was saying, "I am going to get involved in your business. I am going to mess with your priorities. I am going to mess with what you are all about. I am going to mess with what you are doing. I am going to get involved in your life." Suppose that you met Jesus on the street today, and He said to you, "I am going home with you right now." Would you be nervous about what he might find in your home?

It's Personal

I believe that Jesus was saying to Zaccheus, "What is happening between you and I is very personal and very private. There are too many people standing around here that want to eavesdrop." I am so very glad that we serve a God like this. When He deals with us, it is very personal. He doesn't broadcast our issues over a loudspeaker to the public. It's between you and Jesus. In Psalm 51:4, David said, "Against Thee only, O God, have I sinned." God is interested in restoration and healing. He is not interested in destruction and ruin. You need to be very careful who you talk to and what you say, because not everyone that calls himself by Jesus' name is like Him. Jesus said, "Come on, Zaccheus. You and I need to talk." The two of them went together to Zaccheus' house, and the Word of God states that the people began to murmur. They were upset, irritated, and aggravated. "How could Jesus do that? That man is unclean. That man's house is unclean. Why is Jesus going with him to his house?" They didn't understand the unfeigned love of God. Even today, many people don't understand it. We only understand it to the extent it has been revealed. When God gives a little mercy and grace to us, and He blesses us and forgives us, we sometimes put on "religious robes" and we start judging everyone that we don't think is where we are spiritually.

Jesus could have read Zaccheus "the riot act" right there. "I am going to tell you what you have done. I am going to tell you who you stole from. I am going to embarrass you." Instead, He said, "Zaccheus, it's just Me and you." That really irritated the religious people.

A number of years ago, *Time* magazine profiled a telephone line where people could call in and confess what they did wrong. They were receiving two hundred calls a day because people could call in and feel some relief of guilt without judgment because nobody answered the phone. The calls were routed to an answering machine or voice mailbox. Then a second line was added, and there was a charge to call this second line. You could call in on that line and listen to the confessions of the people who had called the first line. On that second line, even though people had to pay, they were getting ten thousand calls a day. People tend to like to hear other people's "dirt." "Well, what did you hear about so and so? I can pray a lot more effectively if you give me the details." The religious people were irritated with Jesus and Zaccheus. They wanted to see Jesus condemn him and rebuke him. They thought that they were about to get even with Zaccheus, and instead, Jesus was going to his home. What an outrage!

When Jesus got into Zaccheus' house, something happened to Zaccheus. It doesn't say that Jesus identified all of Zaccheus' failures, or that Jesus opened his accounting books to expose his cheating ways. Instead, when the unfeigned love of God filled that house, Zaccheus wanted to do something he didn't want to do before. He wanted to be a giver. Romans 2:4 declares, "It is the goodness of God that leads us to repentance." God starts loving you so much, and it gets so heavy that you can't handle it. You are changed, and you are inspired to love and to give. Jesus didn't call him out of the tree with a judge's gavel. He called him out of the tree with a plan for salvation, which results in wholeness.

When Jesus came to Zaccheus' house, wholeness came to his house. Zaccheus suddenly spoke up and said, "Jesus, everyone that I have stolen from, everyone that I have wronged, I am going to give them back four times what I took." If a man was caught stealing from another, according to the law, he had to pay back what he took plus twenty percent. That is all the law required, but when the unfeigned love of God fills you, you go far beyond what is required. People that are living by law are missing something. Zaccheus said, "Even beyond returning what I have taken, I am going to take half of everything I have and give it to whoever has a need." Zaccheus was not looking for fig leaves to hide behind any more. He was looking for people that needed figs! What a miracle of grace and transformation. Zaccheus came out of his tree because Someone loved him into wholeness.

The Joy of Being Found

One of my little grandsons liked to play hide and seek. He always wanted to do the hiding, and he wanted me to do the seeking. He wasn't a good hider at all. Half of him was sticking out no matter where he hid, but I would play along with him. I would go around, and I would say, "Where is he? My, he is hiding so well." Finally I would say, "Where are you?" And he would say, "Here I am!" I used to think the little guy didn't understand the game because you are not supposed to tell where you are. One day, I felt that the Lord spoke to my heart, and said, "Do you know why he does that? Because he knows as soon as he says 'Here I am' that you are going to hug him, kiss him, and laugh together, and then he is going to say, 'Papa, let's do it again.'"

My grandson was willing to come out of hiding because he knew he was going to be loved when he got out. I believe he learned something that many people have never learned. He learned that the fun wasn't in the hiding; the fun was in coming out of hiding and getting loved. "Papa, do it again." It is fun being found and being loved. I believe Zaccheus would say the same thing. He would say, "Do you know when the fun started? When I came out from behind the fig leaves and came down from the tree! I thought I knew what life was all about. I was trying to find fulfillment and success, but I was miserable. Life really started for me when Jesus stopped under my tree and He said, 'Come on out from your hiding place.'"

God had no sooner found Adam and Eve than He gave them the promise of redemption in Genesis 3:15. He put His arms around their fallenness, their failure, and their darkness, and He said, "I want you to know something. There will come a Seed from a woman, and the Seed is going to bruise the head of the serpent. It will take a few years, but I want you to know that the game doesn't end with you coming out of hiding. That is just the beginning. That is when the fun starts. That is when it all makes sense."

Even today, Jesus looks up into our trees, seeing through the fig leaves. He comes with a kind of love that won't rip you up, tear you down, or throw you in the gutter. I am speaking of a love that will heal every hurt, bridge every chasm, restore your heart, and change your life forever.

Choosing to Follow Jesus

God loves you. He wants you to have a personal relationship with Him through Jesus, His Son. There is just one thing that separates you from God. That thing is sin. _The only way to live a deeply fulfilling life of favor and blessing is to deal with the sin problem in our lives._

The Bible describes sin in many ways. Most simply, sin is our failure to measure up to God's holiness and His righteous standards. We sin by things we do, choices we make, attitudes we show, and thoughts we entertain. We also sin when we fail to do right things. In short, to sin is to miss the mark. The Bible affirms our own experience: *"As it is written: 'There is no one righteous, not even one.'" (Romans 3:10 NIV)* No matter how good we try to be, none of us does right things all the time.

People tend to divide themselves into groups – good people and bad people. However, God says that every person who has ever lived is a sinner and that any sin separates us from God. No matter how we might classify ourselves, this includes you and me. We are all sinners. *"For all have sinned and fall short of the glory of God." (Romans 3:23 NIV)*

Many people are confused about the way to God. Some think they will be punished or rewarded according to how good they are. Some think they should make things right in their lives before they try to come to God. Others find it hard to understand how Jesus could love them, when other people do not seem to. But I have great news for you! God DOES love you! More than you can ever imagine! And there is nothing you can do to make Him stop loving you! Yes, our sins demand punishment – the punishment of death and separation from God. But, because of His great love, God sent His only Son, Jesus, to die for our sins. *"But God demonstrates his own love for us in this: While we were still sinners, Christ died for us." (Romans 5:8 NIV)*

For you to come to God, you have to get rid of your sin problem. However, in our own strength, none of us can do this! You cannot make yourself right with God by being a better person. Only God can rescue us from our sins. He is willing to do this, not because of anything you can offer Him, but JUST BECAUSE HE LOVES YOU! *"He saved us, not because of righteous things we had done, but because of his mercy." (Titus 3:5 NIV)*

It is God's grace that allows you to come to Him, not your efforts to "clean up your life" or "work your way" to Heaven. You cannot earn His favor or His salvation; it is a free gift. *"For it is by grace you have been saved, through faith—and this is not from yourselves, it is the gift of God— not by works, so that no one can boast." (Ephesians 2:8-9 NIV)*

For you to come to God, the penalty for your sin must be paid. God's gift to you is His Son, Jesus, who paid the debt for you when He died on the cross. *"For the wages of sin is death, but the gift of God is eternal life in Christ Jesus our Lord." (Romans 6:23 NIV)*

Jesus paid the price for your sin and mine by giving His life on a cross at a place called Calvary, just outside of the city walls of Jerusalem. God brought Jesus back from the dead. He provided the way for you to have a personal relationship with Him through Jesus. When we realize how deeply our sin grieves the heart of God and how desperately we need a Savior, we are ready to receive God's offer of salvation. To admit that we are sinners means turning away from our sin and selfishness and turning to follow Jesus. The Bible word for this is "repentance" – to change our thinking about how grievous sin is so that our thinking is in line with that of God. All that is left for you to do is to accept the gift that Jesus is holding out for you right now. *"If you declare with your mouth, 'Jesus is Lord,' and believe in your heart that God raised him from the dead, you will be saved. For it is with your heart that you believe and are justified, and it is with your mouth that you profess your faith and are saved." (Romans 10:9-10 NIV)*

God says that if you believe in His Son, Jesus Christ, you can live forever with Him in glory. *"For God so loved the world that he gave his one and only Son, that whoever believes in him shall not perish but have eternal life."* (John 3:16)

Are you ready to accept the gift of eternal life that Jesus is offering you right now? Let's review what the commitment involves:

- **I acknowledge I am a sinner in need of a Savior.** This is to repent or turn away from sin.
- **I believe in my heart that God raised Jesus from the dead**. This is to trust that Jesus paid the full penalty for my sins.
- **I confess Jesus as my Lord and my God.** This is to surrender control of my life to Jesus.
- **I receive Jesus as my Savior forever.** This is to accept what God has done for me and in me, what He promised.

If it is your sincere desire to receive Jesus into your heart as your personal Lord and Savior, then talk to God from your heart. Here's a suggested prayer: "Lord Jesus, I know that I am a sinner, and I do not deserve eternal life, but I believe You died and rose from the grave to make me a new creation and to prepare me to dwell in Your presence forever. Jesus, come into my life, take control of my life, forgive my sins, and save me. I am now placing my trust in You alone for my salvation, and I accept Your free gift of eternal life."

If you have trusted Jesus Christ as your Lord and Savior, you are now truly able to experience the joy of living in a personal relationship with God! You are truly blessed and highly favored! Spend time with Him each day in prayer and personal worship. Get involved in a Bible-believing local church and serve Him with all of your heart. God bless you as you enter the glorious new life you are about to experience!

About the Author

Blessed with the caring, compassionate heart of a shepherd, Dr. Leonard Gardner has over 60 years of pastoral and ministerial experience. Often called a "pastor`s pastor," he has planted churches and mentored pastors and leaders in the true spirit of a "father." Dr. Gardner is the founder of Liberating Word Ministries (www.liberatingword.org) and he travels throughout the United States and abroad with a vision to strengthen and encourage pastors, leaders, churches, and ministries. His heart is for restoration and revival. His style of ministry is seasoned with humor while carrying a powerful anointing. Dr. Gardner has four children and resides in Clinton Township, Michigan.

More Inspirational Books from
Dr. Leonard Gardner

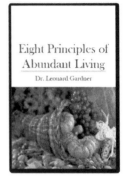

Eight Principles of Abundant Living

In this inspiring and thought provoking book, Pastor Gardner examines each recorded miracle in the Book of John to uncover spiritual principles of abundant living which can lead you into a lifestyle of deep satisfaction, joy, fulfillment, and true happiness.

The Unfeigned Love of God

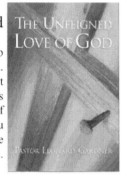

The Bible uses the word "unfeigned" to characterize the indescribable love of God. Unfeigned means "genuine, real, pure, not pretentious, and not hypocritical." This powerful book, derived from a series of sermons by Pastor Gardner, will help you understand, accept, and embrace the incredible love God seeks to lavish on you.

Walking Through the High and Hard Places

Life has its ups and downs. The key to a fulfilling life is learning to "walk through" whatever situation or circumstance you encounter, and to emerge victoriously! The spiritual principles you learn in this book will give you the strength to handle any circumstance in life!

The Work of the Potter's Hands

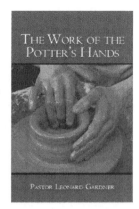

You are not alive by accident! Isaiah 64:8 declares that God is the potter, and we are the clay. This book examines seven types of Biblical pottery vessels and the process the potter uses to shape and repair vessels. Learn powerful life lessons and know your life is in the hands of a loving God who is forming you through life's experiences so that you "take shape" to fulfill your unique purpose.

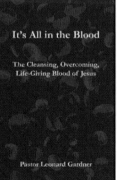

It's All in the Blood

This fascinating book draws intriguing and powerful analogies between the incredible design and operation of blood in the human body, and the life-changing spiritual power and provision that is available in the blood of Jesus Christ.

Like the Eagle

Learn how the eagle's lifestyle and attributes can teach you to "soar higher" in your life, as you become like the eagle in areas such as vision, diet, maturity, renewal, commitment, and living an overcoming life.

The Blood Covenant

Blood covenant is a central theme of
the entire Bible, and understanding
blood covenant will make the Bible
come alive to you in brand new ways.
Learn the ten steps of blood covenant,
the real significance of communion,
the names of God and what they mean,
and how walking in a true covenant
relationship with God can radically
change your life.

Bread that Satisfies

Are you truly satisfied in life? Is your
appetite for God everything you desire it
to be? The aroma of freshly baked
homemade bread awakens hunger in
almost anyone. Learn how to stir a
similar spiritual hunger in your heart for
Jesus, the Bread of Life. Knowing Him
will satisfy the deepest hunger of your
spirit.

Living in the Favor of God

Is your life truly blessed? In this study
of the Beatitudes, you will learn what
Jesus meant by the phrase, "Blessed are
they..." Learn the conditions of God's
favor as well as the provisions that He
has in store for those who desire to live a
truly blessed life!

Chosen to Follow Jesus

Who were the twelve disciples? Why did Jesus choose them to follow Him, and what can we learn from their lives? This study of "the twelve" delivers fresh insight into their backgrounds and characteristics, and teaches principles that we, as those chosen to follow Jesus today, can apply to our walk with Him.

Treasures in the Word
Volume 1

A collection of over 100 "treasures" gleaned from the Bible by Dr. Leonard Gardner over the course of his six decades in ministry, this book is perfect for pastors or teachers searching for fresh sermon ideas, and for those looking for a unique daily devotional book.

Liberating Word Ministries

PO Box 380291
Clinton Township MI 48038
Phone: (586) 216-3668
Fax: (586) 416-4658
lgardner@liberatingword.org

Made in the USA
Charleston, SC
22 June 2013